W9-AOR-103

Microwave Magic
Lunch Box

Contributors to this series:

Recipes and Technical Assistance:
École de cuisine Bachand-Bissonnette
Cooking consultants:
Denis Bissonette
Michèle Émond
Dietician:
Christiane Barbeau
Photos:
Laramée Morel Communications
Audio-Visuelles
Design:
Claudette Taillefer
Assistants:
Julie Deslauriers
Philippe O'Connor
Joan Pothier
Accessories:
Andrée Cournoyer
Writing:
Communications La Griffe Inc.
Text Consultants:
Cap et bc inc.
Advisors:
Roger Aubin
Joseph R. De Varennes
Gaston Lavoie
Kenneth H. Pearson

Assembly:
Carole Garon
Vital Lapalme
Jean-Pierre Larose
Carl Simmons
Gus Soriano
Marc Vallières
Production Managers:
Gilles Chamberland
Ernest Homewood
Production Assistants:
Martine Gingras
Catherine Gordon
Kathy Kishimoto
Peter Thomlison
Art Director:
Bernard Lamy
Editors:
Laurielle Ilacqua
Susan Marshall
Margaret Oliver
Robin Rivers
Lois Rock
Jocelyn Smyth
Donna Thomson
Dolores Williams
Development:
Le Groupe Polygone Éditeurs Inc.

The series editors have taken every care to ensure that the information given is accurate. However, no cookbook can guarantee the user successful results. The editors cannot accept any responsibility for the results obtained by following the recipes and recommendations given.

We wish to thank the following firms, PIER I IMPORTS and LE CACHE POT, for their contribution to the illustration of this set.

Canadian Cataloguing in Publication Data

Main entry under title:
Lunch box

(Microwave magic)
Includes index.
ISBN 0-7172-2595-X

1. Microwave cookery. 2. Lunchbox cookery.
I. Series: Microwave magic (Toronto, Ont.)

TX832.L86 1989 641.5'882 C89-093484-3

Printed and Bound in Canada

Table of Contents

Note from the Editor 6
Power Levels 7
The Lunch Box 8
The Trick to Fabulous Daily Lunches: Planning! 10
Storing Food 12
Defrosting Food 13
Cooking Food 14
Cold Lunches 16
Meals to Reheat at Lunchtime 38
Meals to Cook at Lunchtime 84
All-Purpose Meat Bases 102
Lunch Box Terminology 107
Culinary Terminology 108
Conversion Chart 109
Index 110

Microwave Magic is a multi-volume set, with each volume devoted to a particular type of cooking. So, if you are looking for a chicken recipe, you simply go to one of the two volumes that deal with poultry. Each volume has its own index, and the final volume contains a general index to the complete set.

Microwave Magic puts over twelve hundred recipes at your fingertips. You will find it as useful as the microwave oven itself. Enjoy!

Note from the Editor

How to Use this Book
The books in this set have been designed to make your job as easy as possible. As a result, most of the recipes are set out in a standard way.

We suggest that you begin by consulting the information chart for the recipe you have chosen. You will find there all the information you need to decide if you are able to make it: preparation time, cost per serving, level of difficulty, number of calories per serving and other relevant details. Thus, if you have only 30 minutes in which to prepare the evening meal, you will quickly be able to tell which recipe is possible and suits your schedule.

The list of ingredients is always clearly separated from the main text. When space allows, the ingredients are shown together in a photograph so that you can make sure you have them all without rereading the list—another way of saving your valuable time. In addition, for the more complex recipes we have supplied photographs of the key stages involved either in preparation or serving.

All the dishes in this book have been cooked in a 700 watt microwave oven. If your oven has a different wattage, consult the conversion chart that appears on the following page for cooking times in different types of oven. We would like to emphasize that the cooking times given in the book are a minimum. If a dish does not seem to be cooked enough, you may return it to the oven for a few more minutes. Also, the cooking time can vary according to your ingredients: their water and fat content, thickness, shape and even where they come from. We have therefore left a blank space on each recipe page in which you can note the cooking time that suits you best. This will enable you to add a personal touch to the recipes that we suggest and to reproduce your best results every time.

Although we have put all the technical information together at the front of this book, we have inserted a number of boxed entries called **MICROTIPS** throughout to explain particular techniques. They are brief and simple, and will help you obtain successful results in your cooking.

With the very first recipe you try, you will discover just how simple microwave cooking can be and how often it depends on techniques you already use for cooking with a conventional oven. If cooking is a pleasure for you, as it is for us, it will be all the more so with a microwave oven. Now let's get on with the food.

The Editor

Key to the Symbols
For ease of reference, the following symbols have been used on the recipe information charts.

The pencil symbol is a reminder to write your cooking time in the space provided.

Level of Difficulty

Easy

Moderate

Complex

Cost per Serving

$ Inexpensive

$ $ Moderate

$ $ $ Expensive

Power Levels

All the recipes in this book have been tested in a 700 watt oven. As there are many microwave ovens on the market with different power levels, and as the names of these levels vary from one manufacturer to another, we have decided to give power levels as a percentage. To adapt the power levels given here, consult the chart opposite and the instruction manual for your oven.

Generally speaking, if you have a 500 watt or 600 watt oven you should increase cooking times by about 30% over those given, depending on the actual length of time required. The shorter the original cooking time, the greater the percentage by which it must be lengthened. The 30% figure is only an average. Consult the chart for detailed information on this topic.

Power Levels

HIGH: 100% - 90%	Vegetables (except boiled potatoes and carrots) Soup Sauce Fruits Browning ground beef Browning dish Popcorn
MEDIUM HIGH: 80% - 70%	Rapid defrosting of precooked dishes Muffins Some cakes Hot dogs
MEDIUM: 60% - 50%	Cooking tender meat Cakes Fish Seafood Eggs Reheating Boiled potatoes and carrots
MEDIUM LOW: 40%	Cooking less tender meat Simmering Melting chocolate
DEFROST: 30% **LOW: 30% - 20%**	Defrosting Simmering Cooking less tender meat
WARM: 10%	Keeping food warm Allowing yeast dough to rise

Cooking Time Conversion Chart

700 watts	600 watts*
5 s	11 s
15 s	20 s
30 s	40 s
45 s	1 min
1 min	1 min 20 s
2 min	2 min 40 s
3 min	4 min
4 min	5 min 20 s
5 min	6 min 40 s
6 min	8 min
7 min	9 min 20 s
8 min	10 min 40 s
9 min	12 min
10 min	13 min 30 s
20 min	26 min 40 s
30 min	40 min
40 min	53 min 40 s
50 min	66 min 40 s
1 h	1 h 20 min

* There is very little difference in cooking times between 500 watt ovens and 600 watt ovens.

The Lunch Box

All sorts of lunch boxes can be found on the market, from the very traditional to the more fanciful. Whether brown paper bags or holdalls, brightly colored boxes or the very latest, ultramodern designs, they play an important role in our daily lives. They are filled in 1001 ways on more than 250 mornings per year. Obviously, one should not take these lunches lightly—a great deal of care should be given to their contents.

Eating well when away from the home need not entail vast quantities of time or money. Precious minutes wasted waiting in restaurants or cafeterias, high prices and heavy, and often poorly balanced, meals have forced a change in people's noonday eating habits. Bringing one's lunch to work has become more than just a trend; it has become a way of life. School and workplace lounges are now frequently equipped with fridges and microwave ovens. Microwave cooking enables you to prepare a home-cooked meal in a jiffy, one that needs only to be slipped into your lunch box.

It is much too early in the morning, and a lack of inspiration is definitely winning over your enthusiasm to prepare your lunch ahead of time. Your well-intentioned resolutions come to the surface when it's time to go to the table; a nice warm meal on your plate would have been just right. You won't get caught again! From now on, the microwave oven is your friend and ally. Whether you prepare your midday meal to eat cold, to warm up or even to cook at lunchtime, the procedure is very simple and worth the effort for microwave owners.

For those who do not have a microwave oven in their school or workplace lounge, we offer several dishes that are delicious eaten cold. For those who are more fortunate and have access to a microwave at school or work, we have prepared two very interesting sections: one with recipes for dishes to be reheated at lunchtime and the other with recipes for dishes to be cooked at noon. Thus, lunches for every member of the family are offered throughout this volume of *Microwave Magic.* As well, most of our recipes provide more than one serving, enabling you to prepare lunches for both yourself and other members of your family quickly and efficiently.

Regardless of the reason for eating out at lunch, it is important to ensure that your lunches contain a variety of ingredients from day to day and that you maintain a balanced budget without dampening your budding enthusiasm—not always a simple task. Efficient planning of weekly menus combined with effective food preservation and proper cooking methods will undoubtedly help curb breakdowns of culinary inspiration and ensure that your lunch boxes are a daily delight.

The Trick to Fabulous Daily Lunches: Planning!

Effective lunch planning consists of four steps: setting weekly menus, compiling complete shopping lists, using optimum food preservation techniques and preparing the meals efficiently, regardless of whether or not you have a microwave at your disposal at lunchtime.

Setting Your Menus

Setting your menu does not mean deciding in the morning what you're going to prepare for your lunch that day. The most effective method is to list, on a calendar, your lunch menus for one week at a time. This approach gives an overview of all your lunches, enabling you to balance your diet, your budget and your individual preferences. (Consult the opposite chart to guide you in setting up your own calendar.) The daily amount of time that you will have to prepare each lunch should be taken into consideration. It would be pointless to schedule a meal with a lengthy preparation time on a day when you would have to leave the house very early in the morning; a meal that can be prepared the evening before would be more practical. Planning ahead will make this task easier and you will find allies in your fridge, your freezer and, above all, in your microwave oven.

It cannot be repeated too often: lunches need not be less nourishing than any other meal. They, as well, must contribute to overall nutritional balance, and it is necessary to plan meals that will satisfy your basic nutritional requirements. If possible, consult a nutritional guide, which will advise you as to the number of servings from each food group that should be included in your meal. These numbers will obviously vary, according to individual nutritional and energy requirements. You will also want to take advantage of seasonal produce, both for the sake of convenience and nutritional value.

MICROTIPS

To Reduce a Recipe

To reduce a recipe by half, use half the quantity of each ingredient. To convert a recipe for 4 servings into 1 serving, the quantity of each ingredient is obviously divided by 4.

Be sure to use a cooking dish that is smaller in size to suit the amount required. It is important that the food be placed at the same height given in the original recipe.

If you have reduced a recipe by half, reduce the original cooking time by about a third. For a quarter recipe, cook for approximately a third of the time. Check for doneness from time to time.

Keep to the same method and follow the same procedures as given in the original recipe.

Pay particular attention to details that affect the cooking, such as the starting temperature of the food being used. Foods with a high fat or sugar content will tend to cook very quickly.

Reduce the standing time by a few minutes from that specified in the original recipe.

Compiling Your Shopping List

You will find that your shopping list will be very easy to make once you plan the weekly menu and determine the quantity of ingredients needed to prepare the recipes. And once you acquire the knack of planning for the unpredictable, all your supply problems will be solved with just one shopping trip. The morning when you find yourself short of lunch supplies will become a thing of the past.

Menu Selection

	Cold Lunches	Meals to Cook at Lunchtime	Meals to Reheat at Lunchtime
Monday	Roast chicken and carrot salad	Grilled ham and red cabbage salad	Seafood lasagna
Tuesday	Country pâté with ham	Ham and cheese melt	Chinese macaroni
Wednesday	Pork-vlaki	Tuna croquettes and green salad	Vegetable pie
Thursday	Salmon croissant and parsley salad	Ham omelette	Stuffed yellow peppers
Friday	Omelette sandwich	Teriyaki chicken kebab and vegetables	Quiche Lorraine and green salad

Storing Food

Optimum food preservation is also part of the planning for carry-out lunches. It is essential that you familiarize yourself with proper refrigeration, freezing and defrosting techniques.

Refrigeration
Food kept in the refrigerator must be protected from the odors of other foods. Containers and wrappers must be airtight or should contain as little air as possible. However, as most fresh food will keep for less than one week, you will have to put some of it in the freezer to preserve its freshness. However, with the microwave oven, it is possible to defrost food quickly without having to remove it from its container—a handy, time-saving feature.

Freezing
Food kept in the cold, dry air of the freezer can be preserved for quite a long time. However, if food is improperly packaged, freezer burn or dehydration may result in destroying the food's nutritional value and making it inedible. All food must be tightly packaged in hard plastic containers or transparent polyethylene bags.

Keep in mind that your entire lunch will eventually have to be packed carefully. Experiment with different sizes and shapes of containers or bags so that you can pack your lunch box with ease. Should you decide to freeze foods, do not forget that food frozen in small quantities will not keep for as long a time in the freezer. However, the defrosting time will be correspondingly shorter than that for food frozen in larger quantities, which may be an advantage. Label all containers, indicating contents, date frozen and the maximum storage time (see the chart on this page for maximum storage times).

Food Storage Times (Freezer)

Beef	
Steak	6 to 9 months
Ground beef	3 to 6 months
Cooked beef	3 months
All-purpose beef base (see recipe, page 105)	3 months
Pork	
Ham, sliced	2 to 3 months
Ground pork	1 to 2 months
All-purpose pork base (see recipe, page 106)	3 months
Bacon	Not recommended
Pasta and Rice	
Cooked pasta, without sauce	2 to 3 months
Cooked pasta, with meat sauce	1 to 2 months
Cooked rice	6 months
Fish	
Fat fish	3 months
Semi-fat fish	4 months
Lean fish	6 months
Poultry	
Turkey pieces	2 to 3 months
Boneless turkey pieces	4 to 5 months
Chicken pieces	4 to 5 months
Boneless chicken pieces	6 to 7 months
All-purpose turkey base (see recipe, page 105)	1 to 3 months
Cooked chicken	1 to 3 months

Defrosting Food

Although defrosting food is best done slowly and in the refrigerator, you can defrost food in the microwave if you are pressed for time. You must pay close attention to the mass of the food being defrosted, as this determines the defrosting time (see the accompanying chart on this page). Once you have established a defrosting time, divide it into two or three microwave cycles, allowing for a standing time between each cycle. One standing period is equivalent to a quarter of the total defrosting time. This procedure is necessary because the molecular movement in the food does not stop immediately once the food is taken out of the microwave. On the contrary, the internal temperature of the food will continue to rise briefly. When choosing containers for storage, keep in mind that the microwaves are more concentrated around the circumference of the container and are much less intense in the center—a fact that may influence the way in which you place the food in the container.

Defrosting Times

Food Item	Power Level	Defrosting Time*
Beef		
Small steaks	25%	13 to 18 min/kg (6 to 8 min/lb)
Ground beef	25%	12 to 15 min/kg (5 to 7-1/2 min/lb)
All-purpose beef base (1/4 recipe, see page 105)	70%	5 to 6 min (stir twice or give dish a half-turn)
Fish		
Fillets, in a block	30%	13 to 22 min/kg (6 to 10 min/lb)
Fillets, separated	30%	11 to 17 min/kg (5 to 8 min/lb)
Pasta and Rice		
Cooked pasta, without sauce		
1 serving	70%	3 min
2 servings	70%	5 min
Cooked pasta, with meat sauce		
1 serving	70%	5 min
2 servings	70%	7 min
Cooked rice 250 mL (1 cup)	70%	4 to 8 min
Poultry		
Boneless turkey breasts 4 x 250 g (8 oz)	30%	15 min
Chicken drumsticks, 6 x 115 g (4 oz)	30%	12 min
Boneless chicken breasts, 4 x 225 g (8 oz)	30%	15 min
All-purpose turkey base (1/4 recipe, see page 105)	70%	7 to 9 min (stir twice or give dish a half-turn)
Pork		
Ham, sliced	30%	7 to 13 min/kg (3 to 6 min/lb)
Ground pork	30%	6 to 11 min/kg (3 to 5 min/lb)
All-purpose pork base (1/4 recipe, see page 106)	70%	8 to 10 min (stir twice)

* Allow 10 minutes for standing time.

Cooking Food

Cooking Times

Food Item	Power Level	Cooking Time
Beef		
Ground beef	100%	8 to 13 min/kg (4 to 6 min/lb)
Fish		
Whole	70%	13 to 20 min/kg (6 to 9 min/lb)
Fillets	100%	7 to 13 min/kg (3 to 6 min/lb)
Steaks	70%	15 to 20 min/kg (7 to 9 min/lb)
Pork		
Ham	100%	first 5 min
	50%	25 to 33 min/kg (12 to 15 min/lb)
Ham, precooked	100%	first 5 min
	50%	22 to 25 min/kg (10 to 12 min/lb)
Ground pork	100%	13 min/kg (6 min/lb)
Poultry		
Chicken, whole	70%	22 min/kg (10 min/lb)
Chicken, quartered	70%	22 min/kg (10 min/lb)
Drumsticks, 4 x 115 g (4 oz)	70%	8 to 10 min
Vegetables, Blanched and Frozen		
Asparagus, broccoli, Brussels sprouts, carrots (sliced), cauliflower (flowerets), squash (diced)	100%	5 to 6 min/284 g (10 oz)
Spinach	100%	3 to 4 min/284 g (10 oz)
Beans, corn kernels	100%	4 to 5 min/284 g (10 oz)

The microwave oven has revolutionized cooking by appreciably decreasing cooking times. When faster cooking is combined with reduced defrosting time, microwaving drastically reduces the time required to create delicious, nutritious lunches. The cooking time in the microwave is dependent on several factors: the power level, the type of food, the food's initial temperature, the moisture, fat and sugar content in the food, the presence of bones and their size, and the quantity of liquid added during preparation. Since fat attracts the microwaves, lean meat will cook more slowly than fat meat.

The quality of the cooking depends directly on the shape of the cookware. In a ring dish (or tube pan), for instance, the food cooks evenly because there is nothing in the center, where the cooking is slower. But, as a meal in this shape would be difficult to fit into a lunch box, you can easily substitute a round container. In a square pan the food in the corners is exposed to twice as many microwaves as that in the center, making it necessary to stir or turn over the food more frequently during the cooking time, to cover the food, or reduce the power level. Square pans, however, do have the advantage of stacking easily and can be used to cook meals to be served cold or those to be reheated at lunchtime.

Any material that allows the microwaves to pass through it can be used to cook or reheat food in the microwave oven: glass, paper (paper towel, waxed paper, paper napkins), crockery, ceramic, straw or wicker containers and plastic wrap. Metal containers, containers with metal parts and dishes adorned with metal may not be used because metal causes sparks and can damage the oven. Paper lunch bags, glasses or cups that are not heat resistant and paper containing synthetic fibres such as nylon cannot be used in the microwave oven. Aluminum foil may be used in small quantities to protect bony or thin areas of food from the microwaves.

Cold Lunches

When preparing lunch the evening before, get into the habit of putting any frozen food that you will need the following day into the refrigerator and not in your lunch box. Allowing food to thaw in the lunch box creates condensation and impairs its flavor and freshness. It's better to take a few minutes and defrost the food in the microwave.

Meals to Reheat at Lunchtime

Should you have a refrigerator as well as a microwave at work, you can take a cooked meal out of your freezer in the morning and keep it in your workplace refrigerator until noon. If it is not completely defrosted at lunchtime, you need only put it into the microwave for a couple of minutes to complete the process and then reheat it.

Meals to be Cooked at Lunchtime

The same procedure applies to defrosting food to be cooked outside the home. However, pay particular attention to meat; it produces a large quantity of liquid when defrosting and the juices heat up quickly, causing the meat to start cooking before the center is completely defrosted. Remove the wrapping from the meat before putting it into the microwave oven to avoid precooking the meat.

Cold Lunches

Whoever said that cold lunches had to be boring and colorless? Not so! People who don't have a microwave oven at school or at work should not be penalized. In the following few pages you will see how easy it is to prepare fabulous cold lunches every day—a breaded chicken breast accompanied by a carrot salad, country pâté with ham, pork-vlaki, a salmon-stuffed croissant—no less!

In a rush in the morning? These colorful meals will require only a few minutes of your time every day. Prepare the lunches ahead and thaw them or have the sandwich stuffings ready and keep fresh ingredients such as buns or croissants on hand at work. Refer to your weekly calendar of menus to determine what has to be prepared for the next day. If you forget to thaw some ingredients overnight, you can easily use your microwave to defrost it during breakfast.

The recipes we suggest are simple and quick; organize them as you wish and let your imagination run wild! Adapt your own favorite recipes so that you can include them in your menu calendar. Add a festive touch when there is a birthday or include a special treat to please a loved one. A nice, hot homemade soup in a thermos will warm the spirit on a cold winter day, just as a tall cool glass of lemonade will quench the thirst on a scorching summer day.

Cold meals for lunches that are certain to please everyone are exactly what you will find in the following pages.

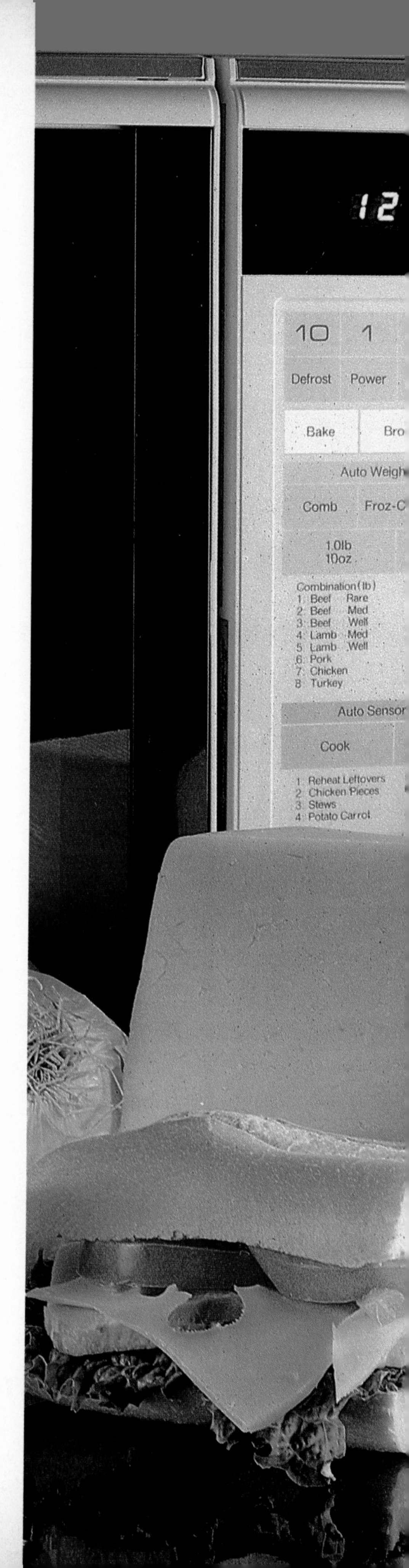

Breaded Chicken Breast with Carrot Salad

Chicken is probably the ingredient most frequently used in preparing quick meals. Coated with breadcrumbs and served cold, it is a popular lunch. This menu is ideal for days when you are short of time; all it takes is 15 minutes preparation time, 8 minutes cooking time—and the trick is done! Accompanied by a carrot salad with raisins, it makes for a highly nutritious lunch. The chicken can be served in a small straw basket, the bottom of which may be lined with a colorful serviette. The finished meal can be placed in a plastic bag and sealed with a twist-tie to keep it fresh. To vary this dish, you may want to add a sweet and sour sauce for dipping.

This cold lunch is a good source of Vitamin A and will brighten gloomy days, keeping the cold winter wind at bay.

Liaison
7 prs
8 tuv
9 wxy
Comp. Abr.
*
0
#
Dernier No.

Country Pâté with Ham

Inspired by our traditional cooking as well as that of Europe, country pâté with ham is a dish that is distinguished by the fact that it appears on practically all buffet and many other menus. Pubs, for instance, offer it regularly on their lunch menus. Its popularity proves that it is always eaten with new-found pleasure.

However, homemade lunches have been deprived of country pâté for far too long; we therefore propose this recipe to make amends. You will most certainly adopt it, as it transforms your carry-out meal into a feast for the eye as well as the palate, especially with the inclusion of crusty fresh bread, strong mustard and a few tasty pickles. Bon appétit!

Country Pâté with Ham

Level of Difficulty	
Preparation Time	20 min
Cost per Serving	$
Number of Servings	20
Nutritional Value	300 calories 16.9 g protein 2.1 mg iron
Food Exchanges	3 oz meat 2 fat exchanges
Cooking Time	27 min
Standing Time	None
Power Level	100%, 70%
Write Your Cooking Time Here	

Ingredients

450 g (1 lb) ground pork
450 g (1 lb) ground veal
115 g (4 oz) pork fat, finely chopped
1 onion, finely chopped
2 cloves garlic, crushed
2 eggs
50 mL (1/4 cup) brandy
5 mL (1 teaspoon) thyme
2 mL (1/2 teaspoon) crushed red chili peppers
1 bay leaf
salt and pepper to taste
50 mL (1/4 cup) pistachios
225 g (8 oz) smoked ham
225 g (8 oz) bacon, sliced

Method

— Place the onion and garlic in a large mixing bowl; cover and cook for 1 minute at 100%; stir and continue cooking at 100% for 1 minute longer.
— Mix the ground meat and the pork fat and add to the cooked onion.
— Beat the eggs and blend in the brandy and seasonings.
— Add the pistachios, mix well and combine the egg mixture with the ground meat.
— Cut the smoked ham into fine strips and set aside.
— Line the bottom of a round bowl with the bacon slices, allowing the strips to hang over the edges.
— Press half of the meat mixture into the bottom of the bowl and drape the strips of ham over it.
— Add the remaining meat mixture and pat down firmly.
— Fold the ends of the bacon over the pâté; if necessary, add more to cover it well.
— Cook the pâté for 5 minutes at 100%.
— Remove the excess fat and give the dish a half-turn.
— Continue to cook at 70% for 15 to 20 minutes, draining the fat and giving the dish a half-turn every 5 minutes.
— Allow the pâté to cool completely before unmolding it.

Cook the onion and garlic in a large mixing bowl.

Add the ground meat and the pork fat to the cooked onion.

Line the bottom of a round dish with the bacon, allowing the strips to hang over the edges.

Press half of the meat mixture into the bottom of the dish.

Cover the meat mixture with the strips of ham.

Add the remaining meat mixture and fold the bacon ends over the pâté to cover it completely.

Pork-Vlaki

Why not give your lunch box an exotic touch? Pork-vlaki is an ideal solution to boring sandwiches, the eternal plague of people in a hurry. This recipe, inspired by the traditional Greek souvlaki, is ready in minutes. Allow yourself 20 minutes and everything will be prepared. Nutritious and delicious, this meal will satisfy those in search of a change as well as those with voracious appetites. Include some fruit for dessert and you will have a lunch with each of the four nutritional food groups represented. The members of your family will also impatiently await the return of this dish to their lunch menu. How easily, and how deliciously, the daily routine can be broken up!

SONY

Pork-Vlaki

Level of Difficulty	
Preparation Time	15 min
Cost per Serving	$ $
Number of Servings	4
Nutritional Value	225 calories 19.1 g protein 2.7 mg iron
Food Exchanges	2 oz meat 1/2 vegetable exchange 1/2 milk exchange 1 bread exchange
Cooking Time	5 min
Standing Time	None
Power Level	70%
Write Your Cooking Time Here	

Ingredients

225 g (8 oz) pork fillets*
4 lettuce leaves
1 onion, sliced
50 mL (1/4 cup) fresh parsley, chopped
4 slices pita bread, 15 cm (6 inches) in diameter

* Pork fillets are thin slices taken from the leg.

Yoghurt sauce
250 mL (1 cup) yoghurt
50 mL (1/4 cup) cucumber, peeled and sliced
15 mL (1 tablespoon) dried parsley
1 clove garlic, crushed
2 mL (1/2 teaspoon) cayenne pepper
salt and pepper to taste

Method

— Prepare the yoghurt sauce by mixing all the ingredients in the blender.
— Season to taste and refrigerate.
— Cut the pork fillets into thin strips.
— Cover and cook at 70% for 3 to 5 minutes, stirring halfway through the cooking time. Allow to cool.
— Chop the lettuce leaves.
— Add the lettuce, onion and fresh parsley to the cooled pork and mix well.
— Place a quarter of the meat mixture on each pita slice.
— Roll each pita into a cone shape.
— Wrap with waxed paper and secure with a toothpick.
— Remove the waxed paper and pour the yoghurt sauce over the pork-vlaki just prior to serving.

MICROTIPS

Freezing, Defrosting and Reheating Pasta

Now you can freeze leftover pasta because the microwave is ideal for defrosting and reheating so that it will not be too soggy or too dry. It is very important, however, to protect the pasta from the cold, dry air of the freezer. You should therefore choose containers that have a good seal; they should not be covered with plastic wrap alone. To save yourself some time, choose round containers for even defrosting and make sure that they can

Mix all the ingredients for the yoghurt sauce in the blender.

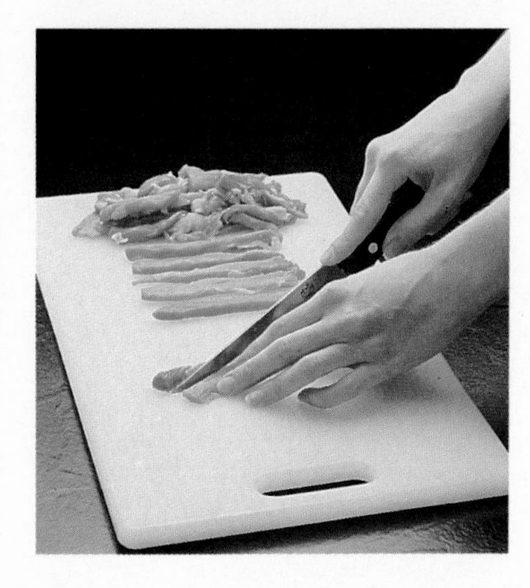

Cut the pork fillets into thin strips.

Stir the meat halfway through the cooking time.

Add the lettuce, onion and fresh parsley to the cooled meat and mix well.

Place a quarter of the mixture on each pita slice.

Roll each pita into a cone shape, wrap with waxed paper and secure with a toothpick.

safely go directly from the freezer to the microwave oven.

Another way to freeze pasta is to divide the leftovers into individual portions and place them in freezer bags, making sure to expel the air before sealing the bags. When you want to defrost and heat the pasta, divide the defrosting time into two or three periods, remembering that the standing times in between and at the end of the cycle should equal a quarter of the total defrosting time. Stir the pasta during the standing times.

Salmon Croissant with Parsley Salad

For a change from ordinary sandwiches, try one made with a light, airy croissant. Croissants need not be served only at breakfast with jam and coffee. Their salty taste perfectly complements creamy stuffings. We suggest salmon filling that is just moist enough to retain a smooth texture without detracting from the lightness of the croissant. We further suggest a parsley salad to accompany the croissant providing a meal rich in Vitamins A and C. This colorful lunch will be a joy to behold, for as long as it lasts. If your children balk at eating the parsley salad, which they will no doubt see as a great green mass, convince them that, like carrots, parsley is good for their eyes.

M à O

Salmon Croissant with Parsley Salad

Level of Difficulty	🍴
Preparation Time	10 min
Cost per Serving	$
Number of Servings	1
Nutritional Value	84 calories 31.5 g protein 5.7 mg iron
Food Exchanges	4 oz meat 3 vegetable exchanges 2 bread exchanges 9 fat exchanges
Cooking Time	6 min
Standing Time	None
Power Level	100%
Write Your Cooking Time Here	

Ingredients

Parsley salad
30 mL (2 tablespoons) oil
15 mL (1 tablespoon) lemon juice
salt and pepper to taste
75 mL (1/3 cup) fresh parsley, chopped
30 mL (2 tablespoons) green onion, finely chopped
30 mL (2 tablespoons) celery, finely chopped
2 radishes, sliced

Salmon croissant
150 mL (2/3 cup) salmon, cooked
1 fresh croissant
15 mL (1 tablespoon) butter
50 mL (1/4 cup) mushrooms, finely sliced
125 mL (1/2 cup) cream of mushroom soup
pinch mustard powder

Method

Parsley salad
— Blend the oil and lemon juice; season to taste and mix well.
— Mix the remaining ingredients to make a salad.
— Pour the oil and lemon juice mixture over the salad and set aside.

Salmon croissant
— Melt the butter for 30 seconds at 100% and add the mushrooms.
— Cook uncovered at 100% for 2 to 3 minutes, stirring once during the cooking time.
— Add the cream of mushroom soup and the mustard powder; stir well.
— Cook the mixture at 100% for 1 to 2 minutes, stirring halfway through the cooking time.
— Gently blend the salmon into the mixture and allow to cool.
— Slice the croissant in two, lengthwise, and stuff it with the cooled salmon mixture.

Mix the ingredients for the salad dressing.

Pour the dressing over the parsley salad.

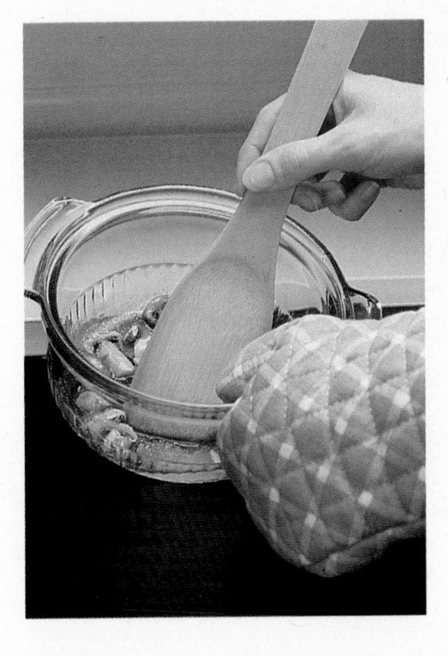

Cook the mushrooms, stirring halfway through the cooking time.

Add the cream of mushroom soup and mustard powder; stir well.

Carefully blend the salmon into the sauce.

Stuff the croissant with the cooled salmon mixture.

Omelette Sandwich

Ask children if they enjoy finding an egg salad sandwich in their lunch box and you may be sure that one in two will pull a face. Egg sandwiches generally have a bad reputation among children. For most, eggs are an emergency resort on those mornings when nothing else comes to mind.

The sandwich we are suggesting has nothing in common with the ordinary egg sandwich except that bread and eggs are among the ingredients. Onions, mushrooms, Emmenthal cheese, Parmesan cheese and spinach join the eggs in our sandwich, giving it an entirely new look and taste. All these fresh ingredients will go a long way toward repairing the damaged reputation of the egg sandwich with your children, and those who do not have a microwave oven at work will no longer feel that they are being punished because of lack of planning. Everyone will love this lunch and ask for it again and again.

Omelette Sandwich

Level of Difficulty	🍴
Preparation Time	15 min
Cost per Serving	$
Number of Servings	3
Nutritional Value	532 calories 20.9 g protein 268 mg calcium
Food Exchanges	2 oz meat 2 vegetable exchanges 2-1/2 bread exchanges 4 fat exchanges
Cooking Time	12 min
Standing Time	None
Power Level	100%, 70%
Write Your Cooking Time Here	

Ingredients

30 mL (2 tablespoons) butter
1 small onion, chopped
225 g (8 oz) mushrooms, chopped
3 large eggs
125 mL (1/2 cup) Emmenthal cheese, grated
30 mL (2 tablespoons) Parmesan cheese, grated
50 mL (1/4 cup) breadcrumbs
15 mL (1 tablespoon) fresh parsley, chopped
salt and pepper to taste
30 mL (2 tablespoons) mayonnaise
6 slices crusty bread
3 spinach leaves

Method

— Melt the butter for 45 seconds at 100%; add the onion and cook at 100% for 1 minute.
— Add the mushrooms and stir.
— Cook uncovered at 100% for 3 to 4 minutes, stirring every minute. Allow to cool thoroughly.
— Mix the eggs, cheeses, breadcrumbs and parsley in a bowl. Season to taste.
— Blend in the cooled onion and mushroom mixture.
— Pour into a microwave-safe pie plate and cook on a raised rack for 2 to 3 minutes at 70%.
— Using a fork, move the uncooked egg in the center to the outer edge of the plate.
— Continue cooking at 70% for 2 to 3 minutes or until the omelette is thoroughly cooked.
— Allow the omelette to cool and divide it into three equal portions.
— Spread the mayonnaise on the bread slices and put one omelette portion and one spinach leaf on each of three slices.
— Cover with the remaining slices.
— Ensure that the sandwiches are well wrapped in order to preserve their freshness.

MICROTIPS

Reheating Leftover Coffee

With your microwave oven you can reheat leftover coffee in no time, without altering its original flavor. All you have to do is place the cup in the center of the oven and heat for 1 minute at 100%.

Brown the onions in the hot butter.

Add the chopped mushrooms.

In a bowl, combine the eggs, cheeses, breadcrumbs and parsley.

Add the cooled onion and mushroom to the egg and cheese mixture.

Cook on a raised rack in a microwave-safe pie plate.

Halfway through the cooking time, move the uncooked egg in the center to the outer edge of the pie plate.

MICROTIPS

Back at Home: An Instant Meal in a Matter of Seconds
Instant meals number among the blessings of the microwave oven. When preparing a meal, divide it into servings and place them in oven-to-table dishes. You can then enjoy a good, ready-made meal almost instantly. Any leftovers can be kept in the refrigerator or freezer. Even when reheated, leftovers keep their freshness and their appearance and in many cases have even more flavor. Make sure that the dishes are well covered with plastic wrap or a lid so that the food doesn't lose any of its flavor.

Meals to Reheat at Lunchtime

Consider for a moment: hot and delicious meals, exactly as you would have at home. Work may require that you be away from the home at lunchtime, but you can cheer yourself with the thought that your lunch will not cause the dismay associated with a hasty and ill-prepared meal. This time you have planned ahead! Your cooking mood on the weekend has resulted in a variety of dishes: seafood lasagna, vegetable pie, quiche Lorraine, stuffed yellow peppers, to name only a few of your menus.

Your co-workers are already green with envy! If they only knew what you have planned for the following week: skewered monkfish on lemon rice, Chinese macaroni, turkey tetrazzini—and more! All these meals can be prepared ahead of time and frozen, thawed slowly in the refrigerator or in no time at all in the microwave and reheated in a few minutes. You are about to see just how useful the microwave is for prepared instant meals. And it will not be necessary to spend your entire weekend in the kitchen: a few hours is all that you will need to fill your freezer and your daily lunch box with delicious surprises!

Seafood Lasagna

A seafood delight that is ready in no time—less than 1 hour from start to finish! Scallops, shrimp and crab prepared in a delicious béchamel sauce and couched between perfectly cooked lasagna noodles. Think of all the mozzarella that you will be able to watch melt . . . at lunchtime.

Prepared in advance and carefully frozen, this meal fits perfectly into any lunch box. Whether you decide to let it thaw slowly in the refrigerator or more quickly in the microwave, you will be able to relish this meal after only 4 minutes reheating time in the microwave. Whether you choose to accompany the lasagna with a green salad and some fresh bread or to precede it with an antipasto and a few slices of garlic bread, you will find this a most delectable lunch.

Level of Difficulty	🍴🍴
Preparation Time	20 min
Cost per Serving	$ $ $
Number of Servings	4
Nutritional Value	590 calories 17.8 g protein 2.75 mg iron
Food Exchanges	3-1/2 oz meat 1-1/2 bread exchanges 2 fat exchanges
Cooking Time	27 min
Standing Time	None
Power Level	70%, 100%
Write Your Cooking Time Here	

Ingredients

225 g (8 oz) scallops, quartered
225 g (8 oz) shrimp, halved
225 g (8 oz) crab meat
1 clove garlic, crushed
15 mL (1 tablespoon) lemon juice
45 mL (3 tablespoons) butter
45 mL (3 tablespoons) flour
500 mL (2 cups) milk
125 mL (1/2 cup) Parmesan cheese, grated
salt and pepper to taste
450 g (1 lb) lasagna noodles
250 mL (1 cup) mozzarella cheese, grated
paprika to garnish

Method

— Sprinkle the scallops, shrimp and garlic with the lemon juice and cook at 70% for 5 to 7 minutes, stirring halfway through the cooking time; set aside.
— Melt the butter for 1 minute at 100%.
— Add the flour, mix well and blend in the the milk.
— Cook the sauce at 100% for 5 to 6 minutes, whisking every 2 minutes.
— Blend the Parmesan cheese into the hot sauce and season to taste.
— Add the cooked seafood and the crab meat to the sauce; set aside.
— Fill a rectangular dish to the halfway point with salted water, bring to a boil and add the lasagna noodles; cover and cook at 100% for 7 to 9 minutes.
— Drain the pasta well.
— Divide the pasta and the seafood sauce among 4 *au gratin* dishes. Alternate layers of pasta with layers of sauce, beginning with the pasta and ending with the sauce.
— Sprinkle each dish with mozzarella cheese and paprika.
— Cover the dish securely.

At Lunchtime

Heat one serving of the lasagna for 1 minute at 100%; give the dish a half-turn and continue heating at 70% for 2 to 3 minutes or until hot.

MICROTIPS

Leftover Green Peppers

Leftover green pepper can easily be stored and used in other recipes or used to bring out the flavor of scrambled eggs, stews or casseroles. Dice the green pepper and freeze it in a polyethylene bag.

Cook the scallops, shrimp and garlic with the lemon juice.

Stir halfway through the cooking time.

Cook the sauce, whisking every 2 minutes.

Add the Parmesan cheese to the sauce and season to taste.

Assemble the pasta and seafood sauce in four au gratin dishes, alternating noodles and sauce.

During reheating, give the dish a half-turn after 1 minute.

MICROTIPS

A Birthday Box

Why not decorate a loved one's lunch box to celebrate his or her birthday? Line the bottom with a colorful napkin. Use brightly colored tape to keep the eating utensils or any other accessories in place. Finish the box off with twirling streamers and a birthday card. Be inventive—make the day a bit more special!

To Separate Frozen Bacon Slices

Heat the package of sliced bacon for 20 to 30 seconds at 100% and separate defrosted slices one by one.

Scallops *au gratin*

Should you have scallops on hand and 40 minutes to spare, we have a nutritious and succulent dish to suggest: scallops *au gratin!* If you enjoy *au gratin* dishes and all the members of your family love them, it will be a pleasure for you to prepare this dish.

Scallops *au gratin* works wonders in a lunch box and makes the meal a veritable feast. But why save it only for lunches at work or school? Prepare a few extra servings and you will never be caught short should friends drop in by surprise!

Scallops *au gratin*

Level of Difficulty	
Preparation Time	20 min
Cost per Serving	$ $ $
Number of Servings	4
Nutritional Value	360 calories 26 g protein 20.5 g lipids
Food Exchanges	3 oz meat 1/4 milk exchange 1/2 bread exchange 3-1/2 fat exchanges
Cooking Time	22 min
Standing Time	None
Power Level	100%, 90%, 70%
Write Your Cooking Time Here	

Ingredients

450 g (1 lb) scallops
75 mL (5 tablespoons) butter
75 mL (1/3 cup) celery, finely chopped
50 mL (1/4 cup) green onion, chopped
1 clove garlic, crushed
30 mL (2 tablespoons) lemon juice
45 mL (3 tablespoons) fine breadcrumbs
15 mL (1 tablespoon) fresh parsley, chopped
45 mL (3 tablespoons) flour
250 mL (1 cup) milk
30 mL (2 tablespoons) tomato paste
salt and pepper to taste
125 mL (1/2 cup) Gruyère cheese, grated
paprika to garnish

Method

— Melt 30 mL (2 tablespoons) of the butter for 45 seconds at 100%.
— Add the celery, green onion and garlic and cook covered for 3 to 4 minutes at 100%; stir once during the cooking time.
— Add the scallops and the lemon juice to the vegetables and stir.
— Cook at 90% for 7 to 8 minutes, stirring twice during the cooking time.
— Blend the breadcrumbs and the parsley into the mixture; set aside.
— Melt the remaining butter for 1 minute at 100%.
— Add the flour, milk and tomato paste; mix well and cook at 100% for 3 to 4 minutes, whisking the sauce twice during the cooking time.
— Season the sauce to taste.
— Put equal portions of the scallop mixture into four small casserole dishes.
— Coat with the sauce, top with the grated Gruyère and sprinkle with paprika.
— Wrap each dish so that it is tightly sealed for storage.

At Lunchtime

Heat one serving of the scallops *au gratin* for 1 minute at 100%; give the dish a half-turn and continue heating at 70% for 2 to 3 minutes or until hot.

Melt the butter and add the vegetables and garlic.

Add the scallops and lemon juice to the vegetables.

Cook at 90% for 7 to 8 minutes, stirring the scallops twice during the cooking time.

Add the breadcrumbs and the parsley to the scallop mixture and set aside.

Cook the sauce, whisking twice during the course of the cooking.

Top each serving of the scallops and sauce with Gruyère cheese and garnish with paprika.

Salmon
au gratin

"Mmmm, what a dish you've prepared for yourself!" exclaim your friends as they watch you eat the first succulent mouthfuls of your salmon *au gratin.* Evidently your meals provoke some envy from your colleagues! To excuse the unimaginative contents of their lunch bags, they will tell you that they don't have the time to spend in the kitchen and that, in any case, they don't have the talent. Nonsense!

You know that time was no great obstacle in producing this salmon dish—15 minutes to prepare the ingredients and 12 minutes to cook the assembled dish. You waited patiently for only 4 minutes in front of the microwave at noon while munching on your fresh raw vegetables and your hot meal was ready! As for talent, any beginner can prepare this delicious lunch dish. Tell your colleagues how you did it—and tell them that they really do not have to spend hours preparing this recipe.

Salmon *au gratin*

Level of Difficulty	[fork, knife and spoon icon]
Preparation Time	15 min
Cost per Serving	$
Number of Servings	4
Nutritional Value	510 calories 36.2 g protein 25 g carbohydrate
Food Exchanges	4 oz meat 1 milk exchange 1/2 bread exchange 3 fat exchanges
Cooking Time	16 min
Standing Time	None
Power Level	100%, 70%
Write Your Cooking Time Here	

Ingredients

1 398 mL (14 oz) can salmon
60 mL (4 tablespoons) butter
1 onion, sliced
60 mL (4 tablespoons) flour
750 mL (3 cups) milk
15 mL (1 tablespoon) mixed herbs
salt and pepper to taste
375 mL (1-1/2 cups) mashed potatoes
250 mL (1 cup) mozzarella cheese, grated
paprika to garnish

Method

— Reserve the juice and break the salmon into pieces, and set both aside.
— Melt the butter for 1 minute at 100%.
— Add the onion and cook for 2 minutes at 100%.
— Stir in the flour and add the milk; cook at 100% for 7 to 9 minutes, whisking the sauce every 2 minutes during the cooking time.
— Add the salmon, the reserved juice and the mixed herbs to the sauce; season to taste.
— Divide the salmon mixture equally among four *au gratin* dishes.
— Garnish the outer edge of each dish with the mashed potatoes and top the center with grated mozzarella; sprinkle the assembled dishes with paprika.
— Cover, sealing tightly.

At Lunchtime

Heat one serving of the salmon *au gratin* for 1 minute at 100%; give the dish a half-turn and continue heating at 70% for 2 to 3 minutes or until the dish is hot.

MICROTIPS

Sharpening Knives: A Delicate But Indispensable Task

To protect your knives and to facilitate your use of them it is necessary to sharpen them regularly. It is very useful to have a knife sharpener, known as a steel. Electric knife sharpeners are not recommended because they wear down the blade prematurely.

To sharpen knives, first hold the sharpener (the steel) firmly by the handle. With the other hand lay the heel of the blade against the tip of the steel at an angle of 15° to 25°, drawing the blade down toward the

Reserve the salmon juice and break the salmon into pieces.

Add the onion to the melted butter and cook.

Stir in the flour and then add the milk.

Cook the sauce at 100% for 7 to 9 minutes, whisking every 2 minutes.

Divide the salmon mixture among four au gratin *dishes.*

Top the center of each dish with grated mozzarella, place the mashed potatoes around the outer edges and garnish with paprika.

base of the steel until it reaches the safety edge. Use a quick swinging motion of the wrist for each stroke. Repeat this procedure, alternating the sides of the blade against the steel, about 10 times.

We strongly suggest that you sharpen your knives regularly, after 2 or 3 uses. For maintenance, we recommend that you rinse the knife in warm water and dry it after each use; avoid the dishwasher. Check the sharpness of a knife by trying to cut a tomato without squishing it.

Skewered Monkfish on Lemon Rice

Perhaps you find this proposal too audacious? On the contrary, this dish is perfectly suitable for a lunch box. In fact, the recipe was conceived with lunch boxes in mind! However, nothing proves a point better than experimentation—try it. After the first try, you and other members of your family with access to a microwave at work or school will be convinced, and you will try it again. Everyone will quickly acquire a taste for this original dish. Skewered monkfish on lemon rice is a recipe worthy of the best seafood houses. In fact, why not complement this wonderful dish with a green salad, a parsley salad or any other food that takes your fancy?

Skewered Monkfish on Lemon Rice

Level of Difficulty	
Preparation Time	15 min
Cost per Serving	$
Number of Servings	2
Nutritional Value	357 calories 36 g protein 14.1 g lipids
Food Exchanges	4 oz meat 1/2 bread exchange 3 fat exchanges
Cooking Time	16 min
Standing Time	5 min
Power Level	100%, 70%
Write Your Cooking Time Here	

Ingredients
1 340 g (12 oz) monkfish
1 lime
30 mL (2 tablespoons) oil
45 mL (3 tablespoons) lemon juice
1/2 clove garlic, crushed
1 green onion, chopped
2 mL (1/2 teaspoon) chervil
125 mL (1/2 cup) rice
250 mL (1 cup) hot water
15 mL (1 tablespoon) mixed herbs

Method
— Cut the fish into 8 pieces.
— Cut the lime into 8 sections and set aside.
— Mix the oil, 15 mL (1 tablespoon) of the lemon juice, the garlic, green onion and chervil in a bowl.
— Place the fish in the mixture and set aside while you prepare the rice.
— In a 1-litre (1-quart) casserole dish, combine the rice, hot water, mixed herbs and the remaining lemon juice.
— Cover the casserole and cook for 3 minutes at 100% and then for 7 minutes longer at 70%.
— Allow to stand for 5 minutes.
— Skewer the pieces of fish, alternating each with a quarter of the lime.
— Divide the lemon rice into two servings, place a skewer on each bed of rice and brush with the marinade.
— Seal well and slide into the lunch boxes.

At Lunchtime
Heat one serving uncovered, at 70% for 4 to 6 minutes or until the fish is cooked; give the dish a half-turn halfway through the cooking time.

Cut the fish into 8 pieces.

Combine the ingredients for the marinade.

Place the fish in the marinade and set aside while you prepare the rice.

Combine the rice, hot water, mixed herbs and lemon juice in a casserole.

Assemble the skewers, alternating the fish and the lime pieces.

Brush each skewer with the marinade.

Vegetable Pie

It's hot outside, and the sun's rays are beating their way into your kitchen. The fresh air makes you yearn to work in your garden, to get back to nature, but the clock reminds you that you will soon have to be at work. There are mornings when this yearning for nature cancels out all else.

Why not bring a lunch to work that will bring nature back to you? A vegetable pie would be ideal; all you have to do is combine diced carrots and rutabaga, corn kernels, green peas and mixed herbs with a delicate sauce and some cheddar in a flaky pie crust. You had scheduled something else on your menu calendar for today, but just yesterday you froze some of these tasty pies.

So, give in and yield to the impulse. Your weekly menu calendar isn't inflexible. Go for it!

Vegetable Pie

Level of Difficulty	(utensils icon)
Preparation Time	15 min
Cost per Serving	$
Number of Servings	2
Nutritional Value	610 calories 20.2 g protein 397 mg calcium
Food Exchanges	3 oz meat 2-1/2 vegetable exchanges 1/2 milk exchange 2 bread exchanges 4 fat exchanges
Cooking Time	23 min
Standing Time	None
Power Level	100%, 70%
Write Your Cooking Time Here	

Ingredients
50 mL (1/4 cup) carrots, diced
50 mL (1/4 cup) rutabaga, diced
50 mL (1/4 cup) frozen peas
50 mL (1/4 cup) frozen corn kernels
2 13 cm (5 inch) pie shells, precooked *or* 1 22.5 cm (9 inch) shell, precooked
30 mL (2 tablespoons) butter
30 mL (2 tablespoons) flour
250 mL (1 cup) milk
15 mL (1 tablespoon) mixed herbs
2 eggs
salt and pepper to taste
125 mL (1/2 cup) orange Cheddar cheese, grated

30 mL (2 tablespoons) butter
30 mL (2 tablespoons) flour
250 mL (1 cup) milk
15 mL (1 tablespoon) mixed herbs
2 eggs
salt and pepper to taste
125 mL (1/2 cup) orange cheddar cheese, grated

Method
— Cook the carrots and the rutabaga with 50 mL (1/4 cup) water in a covered dish for 4 to 5 minutes at 100%; stir halfway through the cooking time.
— Add the peas and the corn; cover and continue cooking at 100% for 3 minutes, stirring once.
— Drain the vegetables, pour them into the pie shells and set aside.
— Melt the butter at 100% for 45 seconds.
— Stir in the flour and add the milk and the herbs.
— Cook the sauce at 100% for 4 to 6 minutes, whisking twice during the cooking time.
— Beat the eggs in a bowl and add a little of the hot sauce to them.
— Add the egg mixture to the hot sauce, whisk well and season to taste.
— Pour the sauce over the vegetables and top with the grated Cheddar.
— Cook on a raised rack at 70% for 3 to 5 minutes, giving the dish a half-turn halfway through the cooking time. For 1 large pie, cook at 70% for 7 to 9 minutes, turning the dish halfway through the cooking time.
— Let cool and seal tightly.

At Lunchtime
Heat one serving in the oven at 70% for 2 to 3 minutes, giving the dish a half-turn halfway through the cooking time.

Cook the carrots and the rutabaga in a covered dish at 100% for 4 to 5 minutes.

Add the peas and corn to the dish and cook a few minutes longer.

Drain the vegetables and pour into the pie shells.

Prepare the sauce and whisk twice during the cooking time.

Add a little hot sauce to the beaten eggs and then thicken the sauce with the egg mixture.

Assemble the vegetable pies and give each dish a half-turn halfway through the cooking time.

MICROTIPS

For Perfectly Cooked Potatoes

Potatoes may not feel tender after the suggested cooking time. They are nonetheless ready to remove from the oven. The internal heat will be uniformly distributed and the cooking cycle completed during the standing time. At the end of this standing period, the potatoes will be completely cooked and tender.

Mushrooms

Avoid washing them in water as their porous flesh will absorb large quantities of it. Should this happen, the mushrooms will not release as much flavor when cooked as one would expect. It is much more advisable to wipe mushrooms when they are dry with a soft brush especially designed for this task.

Quiche Lorraine

Quiche Lorraine, accompanied by a green salad, is probably the dish most commonly offered on pub menus at lunchtime! But why waste precious minutes in a lineup when you can have the same meal at your disposal in your lunch box? It is no longer necessary to convince yourself of the advantages of microwave cooking because your irrefutable ally has just filled your lunch box. It took only 10 minutes to prepare the ingredients and just a few more to cook them. From this point, the quiche was cooked in no time.

Reheated in the microwave oven for just 2 to 3 minutes, your quiche will not need to compete with those being dished out a few doors down. In fact, sighs of envy will be coming from your colleagues in the hungry lineups. And think of how nice it will be to avoid the crowds!

Quiche Lorraine

Level of Difficulty	🍴🍴
Preparation Time	10 min
Cost per Serving	$ $
Number of Servings	4
Nutritional Value	845 calories 66.3 g protein 77 g carbohydrate
Food Exchanges	4 oz meat 1/2 milk exchange 2 bread exchanges 4 fat exchanges
Cooking Time	38 min
Standing Time	None
Power Level	70%, 100%
Write Your Cooking Time Here	

Ingredients

2 15 cm (6 inch) pastry circles
6 slices bacon
3 eggs
250 mL (1 cup) 35% cream
pinch nutmeg
salt and pepper to taste
250 mL (1 cup) Cheddar cheese, grated
paprika to garnish

Method

— Line two 15 cm (6 inch) pie plates with the pastry.
— Cook each pie shell separately, on a raised rack, for 5 to 6 minutes at 70%; give each dish a half-turn halfway through the cooking time. Set aside.
— Cover a bacon rack with paper towel; place the bacon on it and cook for 5 to 6 minutes at 100%.
— Crumble the bacon and set aside.
— Combine the eggs and cream and beat well; add the nutmeg and season to taste.
— Blend the Cheddar into the egg mixture.
— Sprinkle the crumbled bacon over the bottom of each pie shell.
— Pour the liquid mixture over the bacon and garnish with paprika.
— Cook each quiche separately, elevated, at 70% for 7 to 9 minutes each or until the centers are cooked; give each dish a half-turn halfway through the cooking time.
— Seal tightly.

At Lunchtime

Unwrap one serving of the quiche and heat it for 2 to 3 minutes at 70%; give the dish a half-turn after 45 seconds.

Line each pie plate with the pastry.

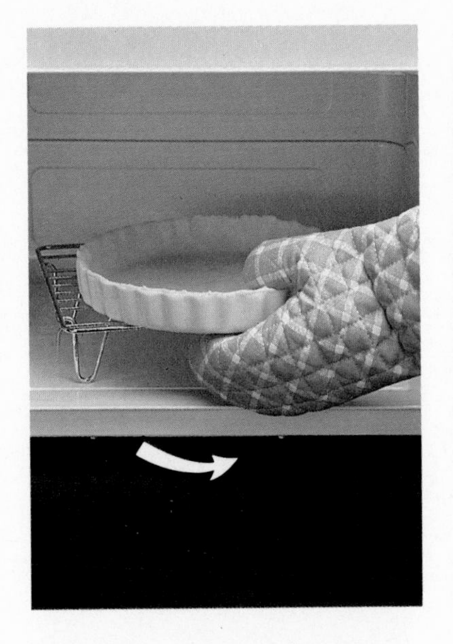

Cook each pastry shell on a raised rack and give each dish a half-turn halfway through the cooking time.

Combine the eggs and the cream and beat well.

Sprinkle the bacon bits over the bottom of each pie shell.

Pour the egg, cream and Cheddar mixture over the bacon.

Cook each quiche, elevated, giving each dish a half-turn halfway through the cooking time.

Stuffed Yellow Peppers

A feast fit for a king! A stuffed yellow pepper, a mixed salad, plain yoghurt garnished with fresh fruit—the first time you put this menu on your calendar, you were not expecting such a success. Everybody loves it! The delicious blend of onions, rice and ground pork coated with tomato sauce and enhanced with oregano, basil and parsley certainly heighten the mild flavor of the yellow pepper. And all neatly tucked into your lunch box!

When the lunch hour you have so anxiously awaited finally arrives, you only have to reheat the pepper for 4 to 5 minutes in the microwave.

Stuffed Yellow Peppers

Level of Difficulty	
Preparation Time	20 min
Cost per Serving	$
Number of Servings	2
Nutritional Value	426 calories 20.1 g protein 3.1 mg iron
Food Exchanges	3 oz meat 2 vegetable exchanges 1 bread exchange 1-1/2 fat exchanges
Cooking Time	15 min
Standing Time	None
Power Level	100%, 90%, 70%
Write Your Cooking Time Here	

Ingredients
2 yellow peppers
15 mL (1 tablespoon) butter
50 mL (1/4 cup) onion, chopped
15 mL (1 tablespoon) parsley, chopped
150 g (5 oz) ground pork
50 mL (1/4 cup) chicken broth
50 mL (1/4 cup) rice, cooked
salt and pepper to taste
125 mL (1/2 cup) tomato sauce
5 mL (1 teaspoon) oregano
5 mL (1 teaspoon) parsley, chopped
5 mL (1 teaspoon) basil
30 mL (2 tablespoons) Parmesan cheese, grated
paprika to garnish

Method
— Cut a slice off the top of each pepper.
— Remove the seeds and membranes; set aside.
— Melt the butter at 100% for 30 seconds.
— Add the onion and the 15 mL (1 tablespoon) parsley and cook uncovered at 100% for 2 minutes, stirring once during the cooking time.
— Add the ground pork and cook at 100% for 2 to 3 minutes, stirring twice to break up the meat during the cooking time.
— Add the broth and the rice to the meat mixture and stir well; season to taste.
— Stuff the peppers with the rice and meat mixture and pour the tomato sauce, mixed with the oregano, parsley and basil, over the peppers.
— Sprinkle the peppers with the Parmesan and garnish with paprika.
— Cook the peppers uncovered at 90% for 2 minutes; giving the dish a half-turn and continue cooking for 2 minutes longer at the same power level.
— Seal each pepper with plastic wrap.

At Lunchtime
Reheat one pepper, in its wrapping (leaving one corner turned down to allow excess steam to escape), at 70% for 4 to 5 minutes or until the pepper is hot.

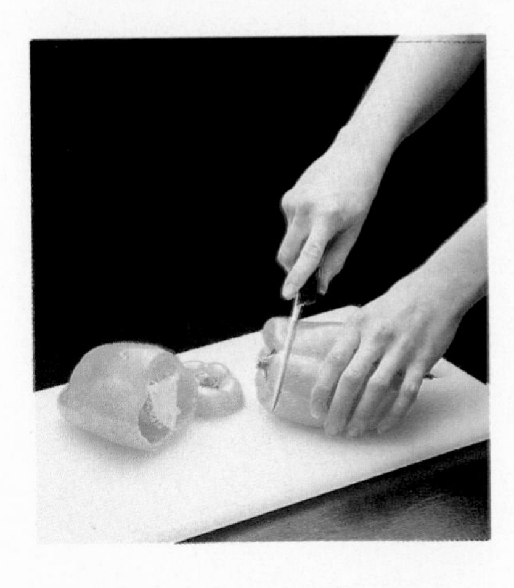

Cut a slice off the top of each pepper.

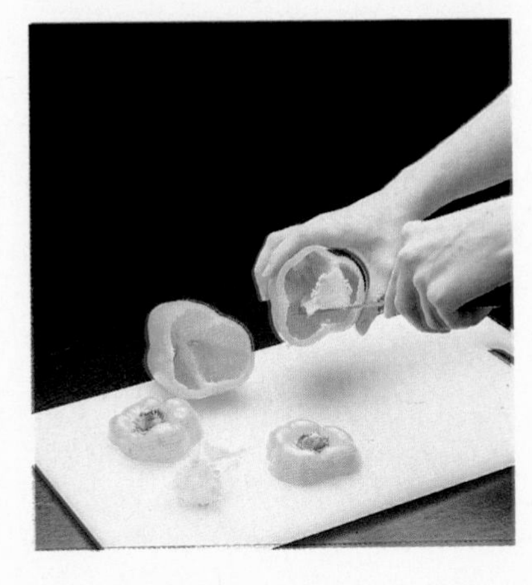

Remove the seeds and membranes; set aside.

Cook the onion and parsley in the melted butter.

Add the ground pork, stirring twice during the cooking time to break up the meat.

Stuff the peppers with the meat mixture and pour the sauce over them.

Cook uncovered, giving the dish a half-turn halfway through the cooking time.

MICROTIPS

Freezing and Defrosting Leftover Rice

Leftover rice can be frozen and defrosted in the microwave, and it will retain all its nutritional value as well as its flavor.

Divide the leftover rice into 250 mL (1 cup) or 500 mL (2 cup) quantities and place in freezer bags. Date the bags, seal them well, and freeze. The rice will keep for up to 6 months. To defrost a package, pour the contents into a dish that is twice the volume of the rice and place in the microwave oven at 70%. It takes 2 to 3 minutes to defrost a 125 mL (1/2 cup) serving and 4 to 8 minutes to defrost a 250 mL (1 cup) serving. Stir once during the defrosting process.

Chinese Macaroni

On today's menu—Chinese macaroni. A dish no one can resist, especially not your children; they will ask for it again and again.

The pasta freezes so easily that you can cook vast quantities at one time. You need never be caught short should your children decide to invite their friends over for dinner. They will have a great time if, instead of forks, you give them chopsticks!

The lean beef, the onion, the green pepper, the mushrooms and the macaroni, coated with soy sauce, combine perfectly to create a delectable meal to carry out. Make the meal a surprise by adding some egg rolls as an entrée and some almond biscuits for dessert!

Chinese Macaroni

Level of Difficulty	
Preparation Time	20 min
Cost per Serving	$
Number of Servings	2
Nutritional Value	330 calories 27.1 g protein 5.3 mg iron
Food Exchanges	3 oz meat 1 vegetable exchange 1 bread exchange 1/2 fat exchange
Cooking Time	20 min
Standing Time	None
Power Level	100%
Write Your Cooking Time Here	

Ingredients

1 small onion, chopped
1/2 green pepper, diced
225 g (8 oz) lean ground beef
5 mushrooms, sliced
125 mL (1/2 cup) macaroni
750 mL (3 cups) boiling water
5 mL (1 teaspoon) salt
5 mL (1 teaspoon) oil
50 mL (1/4 cup) soy sauce
pepper to taste

Method

— Cook the onion and green pepper at 100% for 2 to 3 minutes; stir once during the cooking time.
— Add the ground beef and continue to cook at 100% for 4 minutes; stirring twice to break up the meat during cooking.
— Add the mushrooms to the meat mixture; cover and set aside.
— Add the macaroni, salt and oil to the boiling water; cook at 100% for 6 to 9 minutes or until the pasta is tender, stirring twice. Drain.
— Add the cooked macaroni and the soy sauce to the meat mixture.
— Season to taste and stir well.

At Lunchtime

Cover the dish and reheat the Chinese macaroni for 3 to 4 minutes at 100%. Stir halfway through the cooking time.

MICROTIPS

For Success in Blanching Vegetables

Anyone who wants to take full advantage of the harvest season is faced with the necessity of freezing fresh vegetables. The best results are obtained by blanching the vegetables before wrapping and freezing them. It is important to select the freshest vegetables and to clean them well before blanching. You should also avoid seasoning vegetables that are to be blanched. Salt in particular, will alter the color and texture of the vegetables, often causing dehydration. On the other hand, vegetables that have been blanched are very good if seasoned during cooking; they will retain their color, flavor and crispness.

Cook the onion and green pepper at 100% for 2 to 3 minutes.

Add the ground beef to the hot vegetables and continue to cook.

Add the mushrooms; cover and set aside.

In a large dish, cook the macaroni in the boiling water.

Stir the pasta twice during the cooking time.

Add the drained macaroni and the soy sauce to the meat mixture and mix well.

Heavenly Hash

Do you like potatoes and breadcrumbs? How about beef dishes complemented with onions and Worcestershire sauce? If you do, you will undoubtedly enjoy our recipe for heavenly hash. Quick and easy to prepare, this very nutritious meal will rapidly become one of your favorites. If you have little time to spend in the kitchen, you will find that this recipe takes only 20 minutes to prepare. At lunch, the heavenly hash will be ready in 3 or 4 minutes; you won't even have time to finish your asparagus with oil and vinegar dressing! By including this dish on your weekly menu, not only do you save yourself a great deal of time but you are also guaranteed an unprecedented success with your family members.

Heavenly Hash

Level of Difficulty	
Preparation Time	20 min
Cost per Serving	$
Number of Servings	2
Nutritional Value	440 calories 31 g protein 4.4 mg iron
Food Exchanges	3 oz meat 1/2 vegetable exchange 1-1/2 bread exchanges 1-1/2 fat exchanges
Cooking Time	21 min
Standing Time	None
Power Level	100%, 90%, 70%
Write Your Cooking Time Here	

Ingredients

2 potatoes, peeled and diced
1 small onion, finely chopped
225 g (8 oz) lean ground beef
15 mL (1 tablespoon) parsley, chopped
5 mL (1 teaspoon) Worcestershire sauce
90 mL (3 oz) evaporated milk
salt and pepper to taste
15 mL (1 tablespoon) butter
50 mL (1/4 cup) breadcrumbs
paprika to garnish

Method

— Cover the potatoes and cook in 30 mL (2 tablespoons) water at 100% for 3 to 5 minutes, stirring halfway through the cooking time. Drain and set aside.
— Cook the onion for 1 minute at 100%.
— Add the ground beef to the onion and continue to cook at 100% for 3 to 4 minutes, stirring twice during the cooking time to break up the meat.
— Add the potato cubes, parsley, Worcestershire sauce, and evaporated milk to the beef and mix well. Season to taste.
— Divide the hash between two small casserole dishes.
— Melt the butter for 30 seconds at 100%.
— Stir the breadcrumbs into the melted butter.
— Distribute the breadcrumbs over the hash and garnish with paprika.
— Cook each serving, separately, at 90% for 2 to 3 minutes.

At Lunchtime

Heat one serving, uncovered, for 3 to 4 minutes at 70%.

MICROTIPS

For Crisp Salads

In order to avoid a limp and soggy salad, it is best to pour the dressing on just before sitting down to a meal. Keep the dressing in a clean spice bottle.

Cook the potatoes and stir halfway through the cooking time.

Drain the potato cubes and set aside.

Cook the onion and ground beef, stirring twice during the cooking time to break up the meat.

Add the cooked potatoes, parsley, Worcestershire sauce and evaporated milk; season to taste.

Divide the hash between two small casserole dishes.

Add the melted butter and breadcrumb mixture and sprinkle with paprika.

MICROTIPS

Hard-Boiled Eggs without Dark Rings

Sometimes when you slice hard-boiled eggs, you find the yolks circled with dark rings. This spoils the appearance of the eggs and is especially annoying when you want to use them as a garnish. The rings have nothing to do with the freshness of the eggs but rather with the way in which they were cooked. There are two points to remember when cooking hard-boiled eggs. First of all, be very precise about the cooking time and do not leave them in the hot water any longer than necessary. And second, they must be cooled immediately by plunging them into cold water as soon as they are cooked.

Turkey Tetrazzini

Why serve turkey only on festive occasions when it can be enjoyed all year long? Turkey, like chicken, should be a basic item on your menu calendar; a refreshing change from chicken, it can be prepared in many different ways and served with all sorts of sauces.

The recipe for turkey tetrazzini that we suggest demonstrates all the possibilities that turkey offers. Immersed in a sauce made with chicken broth, cream, onions and celery, served on pasta and garnished with Parmesan cheese, this turkey recipe has no equal. Turkey tetrazzini will recall the culinary tradition normally reserved for the day after a festive meal.

Turkey Tetrazzini

Level of Difficulty	ıİı
Preparation Time	20 min
Cost per Serving	$
Number of Servings	2
Nutritional Value	820 calories 50.2 g protein 8.4 mg iron
Food Exchanges	4 oz meat 1 vegetable exchange 2 bread exchanges 6 fat exchanges
Cooking Time	20 min
Standing Time	None
Power Level	100%, 70%
Write Your Cooking Time Here	

Ingredients

375 mL (1-1/2 cups) turkey, cooked and diced
60 mL (4 tablespoons) butter
1 small onion, finely chopped
1 stick celery, finely sliced
30 mL (2 tablespoons) flour
125 mL (1/2 cup) chicken broth
125 mL (1/2 cup) 18% cream
salt and pepper to taste
115 g (4 oz) spaghettini
750 mL (3 cups) boiling water
5 mL (1 teaspoon) salt
5 mL (1 teaspoon) oil
50 mL (1/4 cup) Parmesan cheese, grated
paprika to garnish

Method

— Melt the butter at 100% for 1 minute.
— Add the onion and celery and cook at 100% for 3 to 4 minutes, stirring halfway through the cooking time.
— Add the flour to the vegetables and mix well.
— Add the chicken broth and cream to the mixture, beating to blend well.
— Cook the sauce at 100% for 3 to 4 minutes, mixing well twice during the cooking time.
— Add the diced turkey to the sauce and season to taste; cover and set aside.
— In a rectangular dish, add the spaghettini to the boiling water, salt and oil and cook at 100% for 5 to 7 minutes, stirring halfway through the cooking time.
— Drain the pasta and divide equally between two small casserole dishes.
— Pour equal amounts of the turkey and sauce over the pasta.
— Top with Parmesan cheese and sprinkle with paprika.

At Lunchtime

Heat one serving of the turkey tetrazzini at 70% for 3 to 4 minutes, giving the dish a half-turn after 2 minutes.

Melt the butter and cook the vegetables, stirring halfway through the cooking time.

Add the flour to the butter and vegetables and mix well.

Add the broth and cream; cook the sauce, mixing well twice during the cooking time.

Add the diced turkey to the sauce; cover and set aside.

Cook the spaghettini in a covered rectangular dish.

Pour equal amounts of the turkey and sauce over the pasta.

Chicken Fried Rice

Our chicken fried rice is a dish that is worthy of your favorite Chinese restaurant. Chicken pieces and long grain rice coated with a zesty combination of brown sugar and soy sauce—a real treat! You and your family will be pleasantly surprised with this dish. Reheated in just a few minutes in the microwave, the chicken fried rice loses none of its flavor and will brighten the rainiest of days. Put a small container of chopped green onions in your lunch box to garnish the dish, adding that "Chinese style" decorative touch.

Savoie

Chicken Fried Rice

Level of Difficulty	🍴
Preparation Time	15 min
Cost per Serving	$
Number of Servings	1
Nutritional Value	668 calories 38 g protein 4 mg iron
Food Exchanges	4 oz meat 2 vegetable exchanges 2 bread exchanges 6 fat exchanges
Cooking Time	37 min
Standing Time	5 min
Power Level	70%, 100%
Write Your Cooking Time Here	

Ingredients
1/2 chicken breast
30 mL (2 tablespoons) water
125 mL (1/2 cup) long grain rice
250 mL (1 cup) hot chicken broth
30 mL (2 tablespoons) oil
15 mL (1 tablespoon) soy sauce
15 mL (1 tablespoon) brown sugar
4 green onions, chopped

Method
— Put the chicken breast and water in a dish; cover and cook at 70% for 5 to 8 minutes, turning the breast over halfway through the cooking time. Set aside.
— Add the rice to the hot chicken broth; cover and cook at 100% for 3 minutes. Lower the power level to 70% and cook for 7 minutes longer. Allow to stand for 5 minutes.
— Combine the oil, soy sauce and brown sugar and pour over the rice; mix well so that the rice is thoroughly coated.
— Put the rice back in the oven and cook uncovered at 100% for 15 minutes, stirring every 5 minutes.
— Break the cooked chicken into pieces.
— Pour the fried rice into a microwave-safe container and add the pieces of chicken.
— Cover the container tightly.

At Lunchtime
Reheat the chicken fried rice in a covered container at 100% for 1 minute and then at 70% for 2 to 3 minutes, stirring once during the reheating time. Garnish with chopped green onions.

MICROTIPS

Homemade Soups in a Hurry

Using leftover cooked meat or poultry, homemade soups can be prepared quickly. For example, in less than 20 minutes and with only 250 mL (1 cup) of cooked chicken, you can make a nourishing soup that will feed four. All you have to do is combine the chicken with 625 mL (2-1/2 cups) hot water, 175 mL

Cook the chicken breast in a covered dish.

Turn the chicken over halfway through the cooking time.

Combine the oil, soy sauce and brown sugar and blend well.

Pour the sauce over the cooked rice and mix well.

Return the rice to the oven and cook for 15 minutes, stirring every 5 minutes.

Garnish the reheated chicken fried rice with chopped green onions.

(3/4 cup) egg noodles, 125 mL (1/2 cup) frozen vegetables, 15 mL (1 tablespoon) chicken bouillon concentrate and your favorite seasonings. Then cook it, at most for 15 minutes, at 100%.

An infinite number of variations can be made on this recipe, using leftover beef, pork or lamb in combination with cooked vegetables, legumes, rice, and so on. A bit of daring on your part will often result in a discovery as pleasant as it is useful.

Meals to Cook at Lunchtime

Why not cook your lunch right at lunchtime, in your workplace lounge, where you intend to eat it? Using your culinary talents away from home requires very little effort—a few ingredients, simple, quick recipes and a microwave oven, and that's it!

At home, the preparation for your lunch takes only a few minutes—merely the time required to collect the necessary ingredients and slide them into your lunch box. When lunchtime arrives, you can get down to business: 7 minutes is all it takes to cook the Teriyaki Chicken Kebab and the accompanying vegetables and only 4 minutes to cook the tuna croquettes. The recipes on the following pages are so easy to prepare that the adolescents in your home will enjoy impressing their friends with a meal they have made themselves—not just reheated, but actually cooked!

This approach to lunch preparation will allow you to savor, while away from home, dishes that are better eaten immediately after cooking, not after reheating. Whether you start by selecting the grilled ham or our recipe for the ham and cheese melt, you will become equipped to add your favorites to your menu list, using all your talents as a chef—without having to be at home!

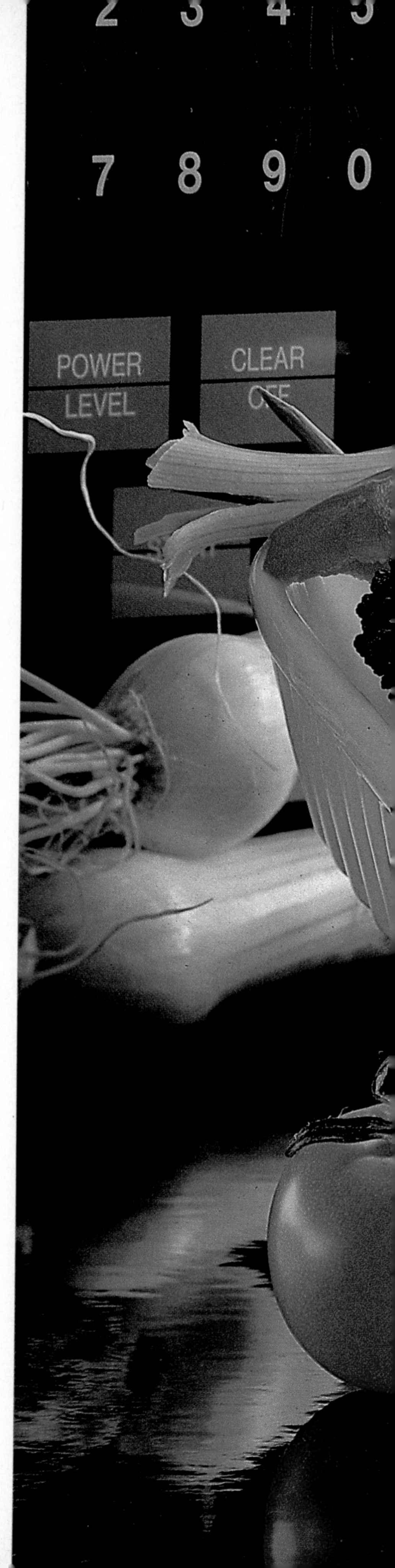

Grilled Ham and Red Cabbage Salad

And to think that so many use their microwave only to reheat food! You have proven that it can do much more. You simply slipped your ham slice—brushed with ketchup, marmalade, green onion and mustard powder—into the oven. Four minutes later, you sat down and enjoyed grilled ham along with a red cabbage salad coated with a zesty tarragon dressing. Your lunch box has left all your colleagues a little nonplussed.

Cooking your meals at work, school or elsewhere is not a difficult task. By following the microwave cooking rules and by preparing simple and quick recipes, your efforts will result in a success.

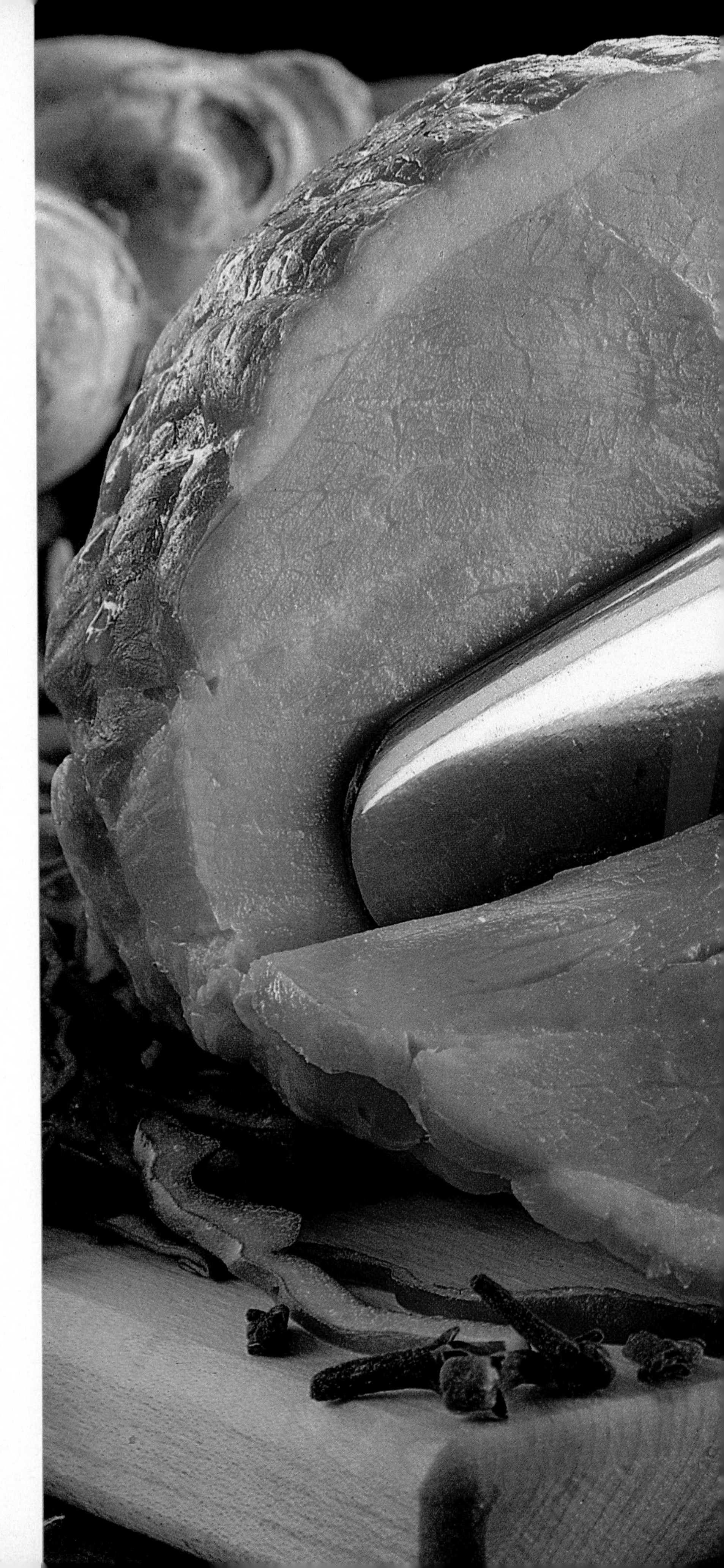

Grilled Ham and Red Cabbage Salad

Level of Difficulty	🍴
Preparation Time	20 min
Cost per Serving	$
Number of Servings	2
Nutritional Value	505 calories 32 g protein 4.3 mg iron
Food Exchanges	4 oz meat 2 vegetable exchanges 4-1/2 fat exchanges
Cooking Time	4 min
Standing Time	None
Power Level	70%
Write Your Cooking Time Here	

Ingredients

Grilled Ham
1 slice precooked ham
30 mL (2 tablespoons) ketchup
15 mL (1 tablespoon) orange marmalade
1 green onion, chopped
5 mL (1 teaspoon) dry mustard

Red Cabbage Salad
250 mL (1 cup) red cabbage, finely sliced
3 cauliflower flowerets, broken into small pieces
30 mL (2 tablespoons) celery, finely diced
45 mL (3 tablespoons) oil
15 mL (1 tablespoon) tarragon vinegar
pinch tarragon
salt and pepper to taste

Method

Grilled Ham
— Make several cuts in the ham slice.
— Mix the ketchup, marmalade, green onion and mustard and spread the mixture over the ham.
— Keep in the refrigerator in an airtight wrapping.

Red Cabbage Salad
— Mix the cabbage, cauliflower and celery in a bowl.
— Combine the oil, vinegar, tarragon, salt and pepper and whisk well.
— Pour the dressing over the vegetables and mix well. Refrigerate.

At Lunchtime
Cook the ham at 70% for 2 minutes; turn the slice over and continue cooking at 70% for 2 minutes longer or until the ham is hot. The ham and salad you have prepared is plenty for two people—why not invite a colleague to join you for lunch?

Make several cuts in the ham slice.

Combine the ketchup, marmalade, green onion and mustard and mix well.

Spread the mixture over the ham slice.

Combine the ingredients for the dressing and whisk well.

Pour the dressing over the salad, toss well and refrigerate.

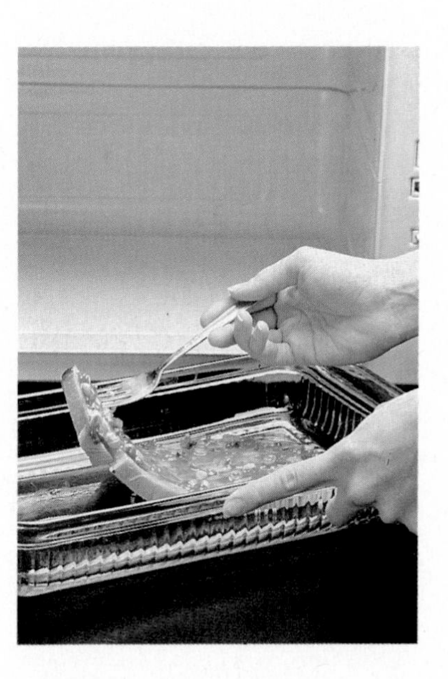

At lunchtime cook the ham, turning it over halfway through the cooking time.

Ham and Cheese Melt

Cheese, and lots of it, deliciously melted—just the way you like it! We guarantee that this sandwich will satisfy all tastes and the most voracious of appetites. The recipe is so straightforward that anyone can master it. For teenagers who have only a few minutes access to the microwave at noon, this lunch is ideal as it requires only 2 minutes cooking time. They will be able to finish their meal, with time to spare for some fresh air before heading back to class. And if you are short of time in the morning, this sandwich is ideal for you as well because it takes only 15 minutes to prepare. You will have your toasted ham and cheese melt in the blink of an eye!

16
New York est le
tion. On y trouve en
marchés qui offrent
mes de première
sonnables. On
moment des
commerces
taux. Ils
de produits

Ham and Cheese Melt

Level of Difficulty	🍴
Preparation Time	15 min
Cost per Serving	$
Number of Servings	2
Nutritional Value	364 calories 17.8 g protein 235 mg calcium
Food Exchanges	2 oz meat 1 vegetable exchange 2 bread exchanges 5 fat exchanges
Cooking Time	3 min
Standing Time	None
Power Level	30%, 90%
Write Your Cooking Time Here	

Ingredients
4 slices precooked ham
50 mL (1/4 cup) butter
1 clove garlic, crushed
1 kaiser bun, split lengthwise and sliced in half (4 pieces)
4 dill pickles
90 mL (3 oz) chicken broth
pepper to taste
250 mL (1 cup) Emmenthal cheese, grated
paprika to garnish

Method
— Soften the butter in the microwave at 30% for 30 seconds; add the garlic and mix well.
— Spread the garlic butter on the four bread slices.
— Place the bread on two microwave-safe plates.
— Cut the pickles into thin slices and distribute evenly on two of the bread slices.
— Place two slices of ham over the pickles on each of the two bread slices and close the sandwiches.
— Pour an equal quantity of chicken broth onto each plate, surrounding the sandwiches, and add pepper to taste.
— Sprinkle each sandwich with grated Emmenthal and garnish with paprika.
— Cover and keep refrigerated.

At Lunchtime
Cook one ham and cheese melt uncovered at 90% for 2 minutes or until it is hot, giving the dish a half-turn halfway through the cooking time.

MICROTIPS

Cooking and Reheating Pasta

The actual cooking times for pasta obviously vary with the size, shape and quantity selected. Fresh pasta needs about half the time or less than that required for dried pasta. However, in general terms, cooking and reheating times for pasta are roughly the same for both microwave and conventional methods. It is therefore a good idea to make double quantities of a recipe and freeze half.

Always ensure that the water is boiling before you add the pasta and keep the power level the same throughout the cooking period. Ensure that the pasta is completely covered with water, otherwise it will not cook evenly. It is wise to cover the dish so that the

Soften the butter in the microwave at 30% for 30 seconds.

Add the crushed garlic to the butter and mix well.

Spread the garlic butter on the bread slices.

Put the pickles and ham on two of the garlic bread slices.

Pour an equal quantity of chicken broth onto each plate.

Top the bread with the cheese and garnish with paprika.

water does not evaporate and to stir the pasta frequently during the cooking. When the pasta is cooked, rinse it under cold water to remove excess starch and to stop the cooking, and then drain well. Add a little oil or butter so that the pasta can be reheated without sticking.

A number of pasta dishes as well as sauces for them are better if made in advance so that the flavors have time to combine and develop. Lasagna, meat sauce and tomato sauce fall into this category. Keep the assembled pasta dish or sauce in a microwave-safe container, preferably a round one, which will allow for even cooking or reheating. It is also a good idea to cover the dish for cooking or reheating to prevent it from drying out.

Tuna Croquettes and Green Salad

You will probably find it pleasantly surprising that to enjoy freshly cooked tuna croquettes at lunch during your workday is not impossible. In fact, to do so is really very easy.

At home, you simply make up the croquettes with a mixture of tuna fish, mashed potatoes and onion, dip them into a beaten egg and coat with breadcrumbs. Then prepare the green salad we suggest to complement the dish. At work, croquettes take only 3 minutes to cook in the microwave and then you may sit down to lunch.

Tuna croquettes can also be served at home, either as the main course or as hot hors d'oeuvres. Served with lemon sauce as a dip, these tasty croquettes will be enthusiastically received by your family and friends!

Tuna Croquettes and Green Salad

Level of Difficulty	🍴🍴
Preparation Time	20 min
Cost per Serving	$
Number of Servings	2
Nutritional Value	565 calories 37.2 g protein 4.2 mg iron
Food Exchanges	3-1/2 oz meat 2 vegetable exchanges 1 bread exchange 5 fat exchanges
Cooking Time	4 min
Standing Time	None
Power Level	90%
Write Your Cooking Time Here	

Ingredients

Tuna croquettes
1 213 g (7-1/2 oz) can tuna fish
125 mL (1/2 cup) mashed potatoes
30 mL (2 tablespoons) onion, finely chopped
1 egg
15 mL (1 tablespoon) milk
15 mL (1 tablespoon) parsley, chopped
50 mL (1/4 cup) breadcrumbs

Green salad
5 romaine lettuce leaves
50 mL (1/4 cup) mayonnaise
15 mL (1 tablespoon) vinegar
5 mL (1 teaspoon) mixed herbs
2 green onions, finely chopped
pepper to taste

Method

Tuna croquettes
— Using a fork, break up the tuna fish.
— Add the mashed potatoes and onion and mix well.
— Divide the mixture in half and form into 2 patties.
— Break the egg into a bowl, add the milk and beat.
— Dip the tuna patties into the beaten egg.
— Add the parsley to the breadcrumbs and coat the tuna patties with the mixture.
— Wrap each croquette separately and refrigerate.

Green salad
— Tear the lettuce and divide between two dishes.
— Mix the mayonnaise, vinegar, herbs and green onions; beat until creamy. Season to taste.
— Pour the salad dressing over the lettuce and refrigerate.

At Lunchtime
Cook the tuna croquettes at 90% for 3 to 4 minutes, giving the dish a half-turn halfway through the cooking time.

Using a fork, break up the tuna fish.

Add the mashed potatoes and onion to the tuna fish and mix well.

Divide the mixture in half and form two patties.

Coat the patties well with the egg and the breadcrumbs.

Mix the ingredients for the salad dressing.

At lunchtime, cook the croquettes for 3 to 4 minutes, giving the dish a half-turn halfway during the cooking time.

Teriyaki Chicken Kebab with Vegetables

We now propose a luncheon feast worthy of the holiday season—the Teriyaki chicken kebab with vegetables, a colorful dish that is sure to delight the eye as well as the palate of anyone who tries it. No one will be able to resist the succulent chunks of chicken and the tempting vegetables; mushrooms, broccoli and cauliflower clusters, onions and cherry tomatoes will be competing for flavor and color.

This dish is proof positive that you can cook your own lunch at work without wasting time or money. After 20 minutes preparation at home, you will be ready to slide your chicken kebab and vegetables into your lunch box. It will take only 5 to 7 minutes to cook. Nothing could be better for celebrating a birthday or some other special occasion.

Teriyaki Chicken Kebab with Vegetables

Level of Difficulty	🍴
Preparation Time	20 min
Cost per Serving	$
Number of Servings	1
Nutritional Value	415 calories 40.1 g protein 4.7 mg iron
Food Exchanges	3-1/2 oz meat 2 vegetable exchanges 3 fat exchanges
Cooking Time	7 min
Standing Time	None
Power Level	70%
Write Your Cooking Time Here	

Ingredients
1/2 chicken breast
2 large mushrooms
3 broccoli flowerets
3 cauliflower flowerets
1/2 green onion
3 cherry tomatoes
1/2 yellow pepper, cut in large chunks
15 mL (1 tablespoon) oil
15 mL (1 tablespoon) soy sauce
2 mL (1/2 teaspoon) ground ginger
2 mL (1/2 teaspoon) sugar

Method
— Bone the chicken breast and remove the skin; cut into large cubes.
— On a wooden skewer, alternate the chicken cubes with some of the vegetables, starting and finishing with the mushrooms.
— Put the remaining vegetables in a dish and place the chicken kebab over them; set aside.
— Mix the oil, soy sauce, ginger and sugar in a bowl.
— Brush the kebab with the marinade.
— Cover the dish and seal tightly. Place it in the lunch box and keep refrigerated.

At Lunchtime
Cook the chicken kebab and the vegetables in the microwave at 70% for 5 to 7 minutes or until done; give the dish a half-turn halfway through the cooking time.

MICROTIPS

Keeping Grated Cheese on Hand
Most people do not particularly enjoy cleaning utensils, especially when it comes to cheese graters. To reduce the time spent scouring, you can prepare large amounts of grated cheese at one time and set unneeded portions aside for later use.

First, buy a large quantity of cheese—take advantage of a sale. Grate all the cheese and divide it into freezer bags so that each bag contains enough cheese for one recipe. Seal the bags carefully and freeze.

Cheese that is grated

Bone the chicken breast and remove the skin.

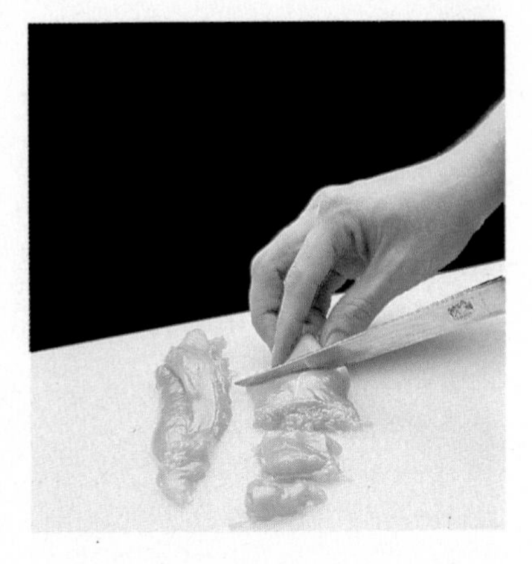

Cut the chicken breast into large cubes.

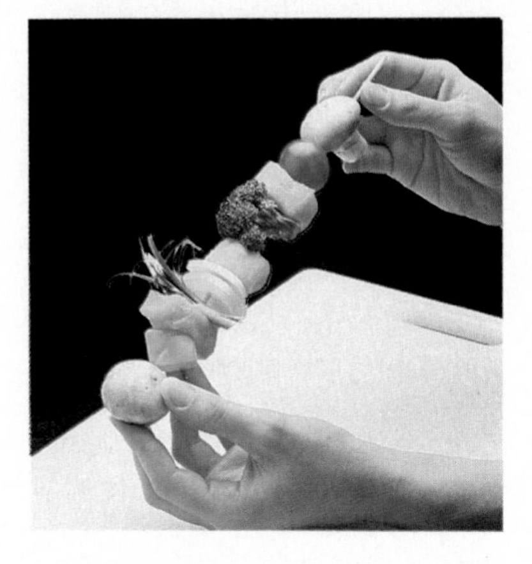

On a wooden skewer, alternate the chicken cubes with some of the vegetables, beginning and ending with the mushrooms.

Place the chicken kebab over the remaining vegetables in a dish.

Mix the ingredients for the marinade and brush the kebab with it.

At lunchtime, give the dish a half-turn after 3 minutes of cooking.

defrosts quickly at room temperature. If the bag is well sealed, the cheese won't dry out and will keep for several weeks in the freezer without losing its freshness or its flavor.

To Wash Spinach
Many spinach lovers think that they must put up with the unpleasant sensation of grinding sand between their teeth in order to savor the unique flavor of spinach. However, spinach can be easily and efficiently cleaned. Soak the leaves in a large container of cold water and gently swish them around with your hands, allowing the sand to fall to the bottom. Then lift the spinach out of the water and place in a colander to drain.

All-Purpose Meat Bases

Throughout this book, we have offered several suggestions for dishes that will help you keep your lunch box filled. We should now like to add to these so that you will have an even wider range of recipes from which to choose. As your time is precious, it will no doubt often be handy for you to be able to draw on the following all-purpose meat bases. These three recipes will allow you, by adding ingredients of your choice, to prepare a variety of meals, to take to work—and at home. Each all-purpose base—ground beef, turkey and pork—provides the quantity of meat required for four meals. They keep well in the refrigerator but have been especially designed for quick freezing and defrosting, with no loss of flavor in the process. In addition, the seasoning agents in the recipes have been chosen for the specific purpose of providing these all-purpose bases with the greatest versatility possible. Use your imagination and create any number of wonderful new dishes by varying both seasonings and ingredients!

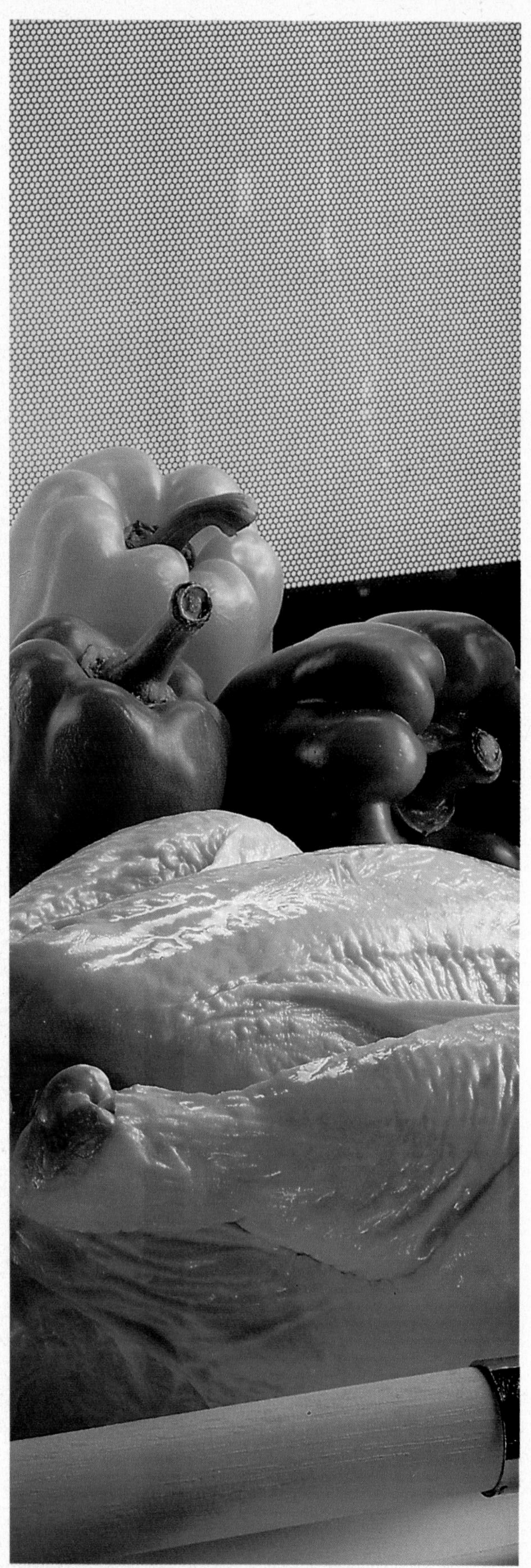

All-Purpose Beef Base

Ingredients
1.8 kg (4 lb) lean ground beef
45 mL (3 tablespoons) oil
4 onions, finely chopped
1 284 mL (10 oz) bottle chili sauce
1 package onion soup
1 package beef gravy mix

Method
— Pour the oil into a dish and add the onions; cook at 100% for 3 to 4 minutes, stirring once during the cooking time.
— Add the meat and cook at 100% for 12 to 15 minutes, stirring with a fork every 5 minutes to break up the meat.
— Add the chili sauce and the contents of the onion soup and gravy packages; mix well.
— Cover the dish and cook at 100% for 4 to 6 minutes, stirring every 2 minutes.
— Allow to cool and freeze in four equal portions.

All-Purpose Turkey Base

Ingredients
1.8 kg (4 lb) turkey, boned
50 mL (1/4 cup) flour
2 onions, finely chopped
30 mL (2 tablespoons) powdered chicken concentrate
15 mL (1 tablespoon) parsley, chopped
2 mL (1/2 teaspoon) basil
2 mL (1/2 teaspoon) marjoram
pepper to taste

Method
— Cut the turkey meat into large cubes, put in a dish and coat with the flour.
— Add all the other ingredients and mix well.
— Cook at 90% for 10 to 15 minutes or until the turkey is cooked, stirring twice during the cooking time.
— Allow to cool and freeze in four equal portions.

All-Purpose Pork Base

Ingredients
1.8 kg (4 lb) pork loin
3 onions, finely chopped
250 mL (1 cup) celery, finely chopped
15 mL (1 tablespoon) flour
1 package pork gravy mix
50 mL (1/4 cup) water
5 mL (1 teaspoon) soy sauce
1 bay leaf
3 garlic cloves, crushed
salt and pepper to taste

Method
— Cut the pork loin into 1.25 cm (1/2 inch) cubes.
— In a dish, combine the meat, onions, celery and flour, mix well.
— Add the remaining ingredients and mix well to obtain a smooth consistency.
— Cook at 100% for 10 minutes and stir.
— Reduce the power level to 70% and cook for 15 to 25 minutes or until the meat is tender, stirring twice during the cooking time.
— Allow to cool and freeze in four equal portions.

MICROTIPS

To Defrost Ground Beef

To save time as well as to preserve all the flavor of ground beef, combine the defrosting and cooking cycles whenever possible. This will work well if the beef has been frozen in microwave-safe containers.

A ring dish is ideal for this purpose. Since there is no meat in the center where the microwaves are less intense, the beef will defrost evenly. If the meat has been frozen in packages, divide the cycle into several stages. The first will allow you to separate the meat from its wrappings. After the second stage, scrape off the defrosted meat and set it aside. Break up the remaining frozen meat and return it to the oven for a third defrosting period.

To Peel Tomatoes Easily

Simply place the tomatoes in boiling water for 1 to 2 minutes, remove them and plunge them in cold water. The skin will then come off easily with the help of a small knife.

Scrambled Eggs

Preparing scrambled eggs in the microwave oven is simplicity itself. Break 2 eggs into a microwave-safe bowl or glass cup and add 30 mL (2 tablespoons) of milk. Beat with a fork and add 10 mL (2 teaspoons) of butter. Cook for 2 to 2-1/2 minutes at 100%, stirring at least once during the cooking. Let stand 1 minute to complete cooking and serve.

Lunch Box Terminology

Baste: To coat, with a brush, the surface of meat with butter, beaten eggs or a liquid mixture.

Béchamel: A white sauce made with milk and a roux (see Culinary Terms). Its consistency can vary to suit its particular use.

Blanch: A method of treating vegetables, by plunging them briefly into boiling water and then in cold water in order to peel, to firm up, to remove acidity or to partially cook before freezing.

Brown: To cook meat or vegetables in butter or oil over a lively flame.

Flour: To coat meat lightly with a uniform layer of flour.

Season: To add spices, salt and pepper to certain dishes to enhance their flavor.

Skim: To remove the layer of fat covering the surface of a liquid.

Sliver: To cut into very thin slices.

Stock: The liquid resulting from simmering poultry, meat or fish bones with vegetables and aromatic herbs in a large amount of water.

Whip: To beat, with a whisk or an electric mixer, in order to thicken and make lighter.

Culinary Terms

Marinate: To allow a meat to soak in a marinade (a mixture of oil and lemon juice, wine or vinegar with seasonings) in order to season and to tenderize it.

Mayonnaise: A dressing made with egg yolks, oil and lemon juice. It is a thick and creamy dressing, often accompanying cold dishes and salads. Several cold sauces trace their origins to mayonnaise.

Parmesan: An Italian cheese that traditionally accompanies spaghetti and several other pasta dishes. It is made with skimmed milk and contains 32% fat. Covered with a crust, the cheese is yellow, crumbly and hard. It is a fruity, yet pungent, cheese.

Roux: A mixture of flour and butter that is cooked and used to thicken sauces.

Vinaigrette: A cold clear dressing, prepared with oil, vinegar or lemon juice and spices, salt and pepper; served with cold dishes and salads.

Conversion Chart

Conversion Chart for the Main Measures Used in Cooking

Volume		Weight	
1 teaspoon	5 mL	2.2 lb	1 kg (1000 g)
1 tablespoon	15 mL	1.1 lb	500 g
		0.5 lb	225 g
1 quart (4 cups)	1 litre	0.25 lb	115 g
1 pint (2 cups)	500 mL		
1/2 cup	125 mL		
1/4 cup	50 mL	1 oz	30 g

Metric Equivalents for Cooking Temperatures

49°C	120°F	120°C	250°F
54°C	130°F	135°C	275°F
60°C	140°F	150°C	300°F
66°C	150°F	160°C	325°F
71°C	160°F	180°C	350°F
77°C	170°F	190°C	375°F
82°C	180°F	200°C	400°F
93°C	200°F	220°C	425°F
107°C	225°F	230°C	450°F

Readers will note that, in the recipes, we give 250 mL as the equivalent for 1 cup and 450 g as the equivalent for 1 lb and that fractions of these measurements are even less mathematically accurate. The reason for this is that mathematically accurate conversions are just not practical in cooking. Your kitchen scales are simply not accurate enough to weight 454 g—the true equivalent of 1 lb—and it would be a waste of time to try. The conversions given in this series, therefore, necessarily represent approximate equivalents, but they will still give excellent results in the kitchen. No problems should be encountered if you adhere to either metric or imperial measurements throughout a recipe.

Index

A
All-Purpose Beef Base 105
All-Purpose Meat Bases 102
All-Purpose Pork Base 106
All-Purpose Turkey Base 105

B
Breaded Chicken Breast
with Carrot Salad 18

C
Chicken Fried Rice 80
Chinese Macaroni 68
Cold Lunches 16
Conversion Chart 109
Cooking Food 14
Country Pâté with Ham 24
Culinary Terms 108

D
Defrosting Food 13

G
Grilled Ham and Red
Cabbage Salad 86

H
Ham and Cheese Melt 90
Heavenly Hash 72

L
Lunch Box, The 8
Lunch Box Terminology 107

M
Meals to Cook at Lunchtime 84
Meals to Reheat at Lunchtime ... 38

N
Note from the Editor 6

O
Omelette Sandwich 34

P
Pork-Vlaki 26
Power Levels 7

Q
Quiche Lorraine 60

S
Salmon Croissant with
Parsley Salad 30
Salmon *au gratin* 48
Scallops *au gratin* 44
Seafood Lasagna 40
Skewered Monkfish
on Lemon Rice 52
Storing Food 12
Stuffed Yellow Peppers 64

T
Teriyaki Chicken Kebab
with Vegetables 98
Trick to Fabulous Daily
Lunches: Planning!, The 10
Tuna Croquettes and Green
Salad 94
Turkey Tetrazzini 76

V
Vegetable Pie 56

MICROTIPS

To Reduce a Recipe 10
Keeping Thermos
Temperatures Constant 20
Reheating Food 21
To Eliminate Food Odors
in the Microwave 21
Freezing, Defrosting and
Reheating Pasta 28
Reheating Leftover Coffee 36
Back at Home: An
Instant Meal in a
Matter of Seconds 37
Leftover Green Peppers 42
A Birthday Box 43
To Separate Frozen
Bacon Slices 43
Knife Sharpening: A
Delicate But
Indispensable Task 50
For Perfectly Cooked
Potatoes 59
Mushrooms 59
Freezing and Defrosting
Leftover Rice 67
For Success in
Blanching Vegetables 70
For Crisp Salads 74
Hard-boiled Eggs without
Dark Rings 75
Homemade Soups
in a Hurry 82
Cooking and Reheating
Pasta 92
Keeping Grated
Cheese on Hand 100
To Wash Spinach 101
To Defrost Ground Beef 106
To Peel Tomatoes Easily 106
Scrambled Eggs 106